IMPACT AND CHANGE

THE CENTURY PSYCHOLOGY SERIES

Richard M. Elliott, Gardner Lindzey & Kenneth MacCorquodale

Editors

BILL L. KELL

WILLIAM J. MUELLER
Michigan State University

IMPACT AND CHANGE
A Study of Counseling Relationships

Prentice-Hall, Inc., Englewood Cliffs, New Jersey

Printed in the United States of America

ISBN: 0-13-451799-7

Library of Congress Catalog Card Number: 66-15285

20   19   18   17

PRENTICE-HALL INTERNATIONAL, INC., *London*
PRENTICE-HALL OF AUSTRALIA, PTY. LTD., *Sydney*
PRENTICE-HALL OF CANADA, LTD., *Toronto*
PRENTICE-HALL OF INDIA PRIVATE LIMITED, *New Delhi*
PRENTICE-HALL OF JAPAN, INC., *Tokyo*

PREFACE

We enjoyed writing this book. We were surprised that the writing was so pleasurable and stimulating. Our intention when we began listening to tape recordings of counseling interviews was to learn as much as we could about the nature of human change. We did not intend to write a book. After many months of listening to interviews we discovered to our surprise that we were evolving an interpersonal theory about how change occurs.

This book is our present, and necessarily incomplete, formulation of that theory of change. In a sense we have interrupted our study and thinking to write this book. Yet writing has been a process of discovery in itself because it has helped us to synthesize and integrate our learning thus far. Further, our understanding of the nature of change has led us to write this book in a particular way. We have sought to communicate a viewpoint about how change occurs by attempting actually to convey the dynamics of our theory through our writing so that the process of our discovery could be experienced by the reader as he reads.

Therefore, we have written the book as a personal document which reflects our own processes of anxiety, discovery, further anxiety, renewed discovery or rediscovery, and finally ultimate tentative integration. We have repeated this cyclic process many times both in evolving the theory and in writing about it. If we have written as we have intended, then the reader, as he thinks and feels about his own experiences as a person who relates to other persons, may well experience the same cycle.

We have been influenced by many people—parents, teachers, clients, colleagues, and many other significant persons. We are indebted to each of these persons for their contributions to our understanding of human behavior. Our ability to formulate our theory as we have, necessarily derives in part from our experiences with them.

Since we have written about a theory of human change, then, in a general sense, we assume this book can be useful to any person who has responsibility for those who seek assistance in changing themselves. Professional persons in educational, clinical, or industrial settings who take direct responsibility for developing relationships which are intended to produce change in others may find this book useful. These persons may have many professional titles, e.g., counselor, personnel worker, psychologist, or social worker. We also think that observers or students of human change, as well as the professional practitioner, may find some of our ideas helpful in understanding some of the processes of human development better.

Many persons are involved in the writing of a book. We wish especially to thank our wives and children for being understanding, involved, and most supportive through all of our process of discovery. Many of our colleagues at the Counseling Center, Michigan State University, have contributed their skills as practitioners and their insights into human behavior. Many clients, our own and those of our colleagues, have taught us about human change by being themselves. Dr. Martha Andrews, while she was with us as a student, helped substantially through critical comment as well as by assisting in preparation of the manuscript. Mrs. Judy Gavaldon acted as our secretary during earlier drafts as well as the final draft of the manuscript.

B.L.K.
W.J.M.

CONTENTS

THE PROCESS OF COUNSELING:

The Dynamics of Human Change

I

INTRODUCTION TO THE DYNAMICS OF CHANGE

Chapter 1

This book is a study of the ways in which two people affect each other therapeutically in their face-to-face interactions. Although it may be true that persons are changed in some manner by every human encounter, we are going to describe the ways in which we think they can and do influence each other during the course of a counseling relationship. While we believe that psychotherapeutic operations are complex, we also believe that these processes can be understood, described, and communicated to others.

Our conviction that the counseling process can be communicated arose out of our working together and led to the writing of this book. We began this project with no clear idea of what the outcome would be. We were motivated mainly by curiosity as to why some people changed during the course of counseling while others did not. What was responsible for these changes? More precisely, we wondered about what occurred in the process of counseling that motivated some persons to give up their usual behaviors in order to seek new ways of relating to others.

We started this project by spending many hundreds of hours in listening to tape recordings of therapeutic counseling interviews drawn from a number of different cases. We followed the progress of the clients throughout the course of their contacts with their counselors. What we were seeking to find were some recurring themes in the process which might serve as clues to revealing what the clients' problems were and what client and counselor behaviors made the difference in whether clients changed. Our own experiences and the theories of others provided us with some ideas concerning what these behaviors might be. But we attempted to free ourselves from prior convictions and to delay premature hypothesizing about the meanings of events until the evidence seemed overwhelming.

At first we attempted to understand how clients changed during counseling by listening to the language that the clients were using, but we had little success when we limited ourselves in this way. More satisfactory results were obtained by utilizing inferences gleaned from client attitudes and feelings and by regarding the clients' words as manifestations of deeper meanings, but this procedure was no more helpful in formulating a theory of therapeutic change. By broadening the base of our operations to include inferences and deeper meanings, we became better diagnosticians; but we were no closer to understanding how change occurs. In the course of our listening we heard the same kinds of client dynamics expressed in the same way with different counselors, and in some cases the clients improved and in other cases they did not.

We then thought that if we could make sense out of the behavior and words of the counselor we might be able to discover why persons change. We sought to differentiate between counselors whose clients reflected a behavior change from those whose clients did not on such grounds as differing counselor needs and dynamics. Here again, we became quite sensitive to how counselors defend themselves in their relationships, what their needs are, how their own problems are expressed, and how these problems interfere with their counseling. Yet our approach was disappointing as a way of studying therapeutic change. Through these two procedures we had increased our understanding of counselors and clients, but we weren't really any closer to understanding how change occurs.

Our failure to understand therapeutic change by studying the separate behaviors of the counselor or the client suggested to us that change must be a function of a complex interplay of client and counselor dynamics. Interestingly enough, although we began this study with the idea that the essence of therapeutic change may lie in the interaction between counselor and client, we avoided examining this dimension for a long period. We think we approached other ways of following the course of counseling first because the task of assessing change by studying the interaction process seemed overwhelming. We felt that the subtleties and the complexities of a therapeutic relationship would increase in unmanageable proportions with each interaction and that our efforts to understand would fail. We were also threatened by the prospect that the interaction might be so specific to each pair of participants that we would not find any basis for generalization.

RECIPROCAL RELATIONSHIP PHENOMENA

The relationship phenomena in counseling are complex and subtle, but tractable. As we continued to study the interpersonal interaction, we discovered a number of identifiable recurrent themes which seemed to differentiate those relationships in which clients changed from those in which they did not. We have been able to organize these thema into generalized statements of the events in counseling relationships that are critical to client change. Although our constructs may also be descriptive of the ways in which people communicate with each other in general, they are particularly useful in theorizing about how change occurs during counseling.

We have developed our ideas about the ways that clients change in terms of the dynamic consequences of the counselor-client interaction in the relationship. Our constructs reflect both the reciprocal impact of their communication on each other and the lengths to which both participants may go to keep the communication intact so that the counselor may be helpful. This communication goes on simultaneously at a number of different levels, and the meanings that are communicated arise out of the immediate stimulation of the given interview. In addition, the participants' communication at any given time also has latent effects which may only become clear in later interviews. We have noticed, too, that the communication takes on a number of meanings which vary with the client's particular problems, his past experiences, and the nature of the current relationship. Further, interaction between the counselor and the client in the current relationship affects not only the choice of content in the interview but even the sequence of the content. Communication, we propose, can break down and be revitalized; client and counselor can destroy and restore a relationship. We believe that the relationship is resilient and that communication problems are reparable. The process of reparation can take place through supervision or even from the client if necessary.

We have isolated, then, a number of factors that are interrelated and that are significant to the process of client change. In the remainder of this chapter we will specify these factors and weave them together in the way in which we have observed them occur in interviews. In later chapters we will amplify these aspects of the relationship and show more fully how they are productive of change, using case material where it seems appropriate. We will also demonstrate how supervision can have a catalytic effect on the process of counseling.

Levels of Communication

We noted early in our study of interview material that the counselor and client were affecting each other at a number of different levels during their behavioral interaction. We found that while the interaction had meaning for and could be attached to the behavior of the participants in terms of their current interaction, richer meaning could be derived if associations were also made to past exchanges. In other words, the behavioral interchange of the counselor and client has residual as well as immediate meaning, and we have found that both meanings need to be assessed in order to understand how change occurs.

By studying both the immediate and latent effects of the interaction we can more closely approximate the meaning of the therapeutic encounter. In their interaction, the counselor and client are governed in part by the explicit content of the exchange. In addition, however, we believe that the impact of their exchange is being experienced at a number of other levels and that the latent effect of this experiencing is productive of and determines in part the content of later encounters.

Besides the phenomena of immediacy and latency in the communication process, we have found that the content in the counseling relationship is determined in a particular way by the interaction. At one level whatever is talked about refers to the client's past behavior, but the very choice of the content of the interview reflects the nature of the present relationship. To understand the counseling process, the counselor needs to examine his own previous behaviors which have triggered the client's thoughts, feelings, and affective changes. For example, if there is an affect change in an interview, the change must be understood in terms of what has transpired between the client and the counselor in that interview and in previous interviews.

The nature of the interaction affords the stimulation which leads to the client's choice of content, both as to its kind and quality, and even to the sequence with which the content is chosen. That is, if a counselor responds to something that the client is doing, saying, or feeling in a manner which the client perceives as punitive, then we have noticed that often in the next few minutes the client will begin to bring content out of his past experiences which deals with episodes, relationships, or experiences where he felt punished. This is an important aspect of the therapeutic interaction because we are suggesting that the sequence of events is determined by the nature of the therapeutic encounter.

Not only is the counselor able to utilize the past and present content of the client's remarks in attempting to resolve the client's problems, but he can also study the sequence of events to better understand the kinds of occurrences that trigger particular dynamics in the client. We believe that this interpersonal stimulation begins at the time of the first interview and that we can learn to predict much about the nature of the eventual course of the relationship from these very early interactions.

In other words, to understand how the communication process influences client change, both the immediate effects of the current interaction and the more subtle residual effects must be taken into account. We not only think that the less subtle effects are available for study, but that unless their implications are carefully examined by the counselor, change may not occur. Later, we will make more explicit how the content of the interviews is determined in part by the nature of earlier encounters and how the climate of any given interview may mirror previous encounters.

We are proposing that if the counselor listens carefully to the client's response patterns at any given time he will often be able to recall in retrospect what it was that he did to set off the patterns. Through this process, the counselor will be able to learn something about the dynamic consequences of his own behaviors in terms of a particular client's expression of his problems. Looking at the counseling relationship in this way leads to the conclusion that, to a certain extent at least, mistakes are impossible. Whatever the counselor stimulates in the client—hostility, hurt, guilt, or whatever—can be utilized in learning more about the client and can be incorporated by the counselor as a part of the process of helping the client to change.

When we speak of the counselor listening carefully, we are thinking about the counselor's experience with this client being available to him in particular ways. We propose that if the counselor looks at the behavior of his client as a probable consequence of his own behavior and if he views his own behavior as the force that may activate his client's responses, then he can understand how the client's behavior reflects the unfolding and revealing of the client's basic problem as an interpersonal process. Further, he can better appreciate how the client developed his particular problems and how their interaction has triggered their expression and the client's accompanying feelings and concerns.

When the client begins to experience some of the feelings that he has defended against, his projections, accusations, and anxiety may substantially increase. The counselor must recognize that the increased client agitation is a critical incident along the path of the client's changing and that the client's awareness of disorganizing feelings is precipitating the client's responses to him. Unless the counselor keeps in mind that the reason for his participating in the relationship is precisely to trigger this type of response pattern and that this is a necessary antecedent to client change, he may become unduly guilty, overwhelmed, threatened, or inadequate in the relationship. Such feelings, although they may inhibit the counselor and retard progress, can also be useful to the counselor provided that he not only can identify the feelings, but can also understand what occurred in the relationship that stimulated these feelings in him.

CLIENT INTENTIONS

We have thought about the ways that clients stimulate counselors in terms of the concept of eliciting behaviors. Functionally, this concept refers to a relationship phenomenon in which the client tries to elicit behavioral responses from the counselor in particular ways and for various reasons. These eliciting behaviors are notable for their significance as a source of understanding the nature of the client's problems and for learning more about the ways in which the client copes with his interpersonal environment. The interpersonal quality of these behaviors suggests that they stem from ways that the clients have learned to behave in earlier relationships with such significant persons as parents and siblings. We have found that eliciting behaviors occur immediately in a counseling relationship and continue in one form or another throughout the relationship.

Clients have a large repertoire of eliciting behaviors, and the behaviors are many-faceted. The interpersonal expressions of the behaviors will vary and are governed by the reciprocal impact of the counselor and client in a particular relationship. Depending upon the nature of the client's problems, his eliciting behaviors may differ in the kinds, intensity, and rigidity with which he utilizes these behaviors.

Eliciting behaviors have two contradictory intents: clients use these behaviors to keep from changing or to get the help they need. Since the essential character of the eliciting behavior resides in the ambivalent intention of the client to further or stalemate the relationship, the actual behaviors utilized by the client will vary with the interpersonal impact that he intends to have on his counselor at a particular point in time. Looked at in this way, eliciting behaviors must be regarded from the intention of the client. In accord with the client's ambivalent intention, the client's eliciting behaviors continue to have both facilitating and impeding effects on the counseling relationship throughout its course. The healthy motivation of the client will continue to operate to keep the relationship alive and moving; on the other hand, critical incidents will occur at those points where the counselor is confronted with the client's contradictory intent to destroy the relationship.

Because of his ambivalence about changing, a client will continually attempt to elicit responses from the counselor which are intended to immobilize him or activate him. At those times when the client intends to frustrate or distract the counselor, the counselor needs to examine the client's behavior very carefully for possible clues concerning the characteristic ways that the client copes with threat from significant persons. If these behaviors are understood by the counselor, they will provide him with clues as to how he can counter with other behaviors which will eventually help the client to acquire a more adaptive response pattern.

The eliciting behaviors which are interpersonally destructive are coping methods which have become ineffective. It follows that the counselor should respond in ways which will not reinforce these ineffective behaviors. The counselor needs to assume that these eliciting behaviors have a defensive value, and that they are the interpersonal screens that the client typically uses to protect his real feelings from expression when threatened by significant persons. The feelings being warded off are the core of the client's problems, and the eliciting behaviors the client utilizes are the interpersonal coping methods which help him to defend against the pain associated with the past interpersonally hurtful experiences.

Thus, clients try to elicit counselor behaviors which will not expose these painful feelings. All the behavioral manifestations which accompany the verbal statements of the client—the affect, content, and manner of expression—are intended to convince the counselor to respond in certain ways. If the counselor's response is inappropriate, the behaviors have served their defensive purpose of keeping the client and counselor apart in terms of any meaningful relationship. As the relationship progresses appropriately and the counselor becomes an increasingly significant person, the participants will move closer to the client's painful, conflicted experience. When this occurs, the intensity with which the client utilizes defensive eliciting behaviors will increase substantially.

The eliciting behaviors of the client vary with the kinds of feelings that he is guarding against expressing. The client may attempt to elicit sympathy or understanding from a counselor to maintain the feeling that he is fragile. Or again, the client may threaten the counselor with certain behaviors if the counselor does not yield to his wishes. In this way, when the behaviors have defensive value, their purpose is to serve as a protective shield against experiencing deeper feelings of loss, deprivation, or trauma.

One of the difficulties in countering the client's eliciting behaviors is that the feelings subsumed under these behaviors are very powerful and demanding, and it is very easy for the counselor to believe that when he does not respond to a client's demands he will have committed a therapeutic error. The kind of error that the counselor thinks he has committed will depend upon the variety, the intensity, and the nature of the eliciting forces of the client's behaviors. These behaviors may variously stimulate the counselor to feel guilty, inadequate, omnipotent, or narcissistic. How vulnerable the counselor is to responding to the defensive value of the eliciting behaviors depends upon the nature of his own dynamics, needs, and defenses. No counselor is invulnerable; in fact the counselor's vulnerability can be productive of therapeutic progress if the counselor can convert the dynamic, interpersonal consequences of his own less than perfect behavior into corrective measures in the counseling hour.

If the counselor does stir the genuine feelings subsumed under the client's defensive eliciting behaviors, we have found that this success may stimulate the client to present other eliciting behaviors which are alternative ways the client has learned to defend against change. These alternative eliciting behaviors may deceive the counselor into believing that he has effected a behavioral change when in fact these behaviors may only represent another side of the client's defensive coping against change. The range of alternative eliciting behaviors available to the client reflects his developmental patterns and the ways that he has learned to cope with his family and significant others.

Healthy and Destructive Resistances

The consequence of what the client achieves with his eliciting behaviors will have any one of a number of effects on that relationship. If the client has been unsuccessful in stimulating the counselor to behave in ways that are therapeutically unproductive, then the client may tend to search for new methods of coping with the counselor. All of these ways utilized by the client to deter the counselor from his purpose of helping him to change can be called resistance in the negative sense.

However, in the preceding section we also indicated that the client can utilize eliciting behaviors to enhance and further the relationship. What we are suggesting is that resistance is not solely a function of the client's unwillingness or inability to change. On the contrary, we have repeatedly observed ways in which the counselor has resisted the client's willingness to change because of his own needs or conflicts. Whenever the client attempts to elicit responses from the counselor which are intended to help the counselor and further the relationship, we have called this "healthy" resistance.

Although the client's healthy and defensive resistances can be explained in terms of the eliciting behaviors without invoking a new concept, there are some useful dimensions of the relationship that can be explained more easily with this concept. If the client's behaviors are a protective shield against his real feelings and the counselor is deceived into believing that he is assisting the client whereas he is really helping the client defend against his conflicted feelings, then the client will exhibit what we have chosen to call healthy resistance. If, on the other hand, the eliciting behaviors have resulted in an appropriate therapeutic response from the counselor, then the client is likely to resort to defensive resistance and to further eliciting behaviors which will attempt to distract and confuse the counselor.

Since we view the concept of resistance as applying equally well to both client and counselor, we will elaborate on this concept in another fashion, utilizing the notion of ambivalence. Although the purpose of counseling is to change peoples' behavior because they wish to be changed, the course of counseling is not easy because the wish to change is ambivalently experienced. The undesirable behavior is accompanied by sufficient gain to make the prospect of giving it up for uncertain rewards a difficult process at best. So people enter the counseling relationship with mixed feelings about wanting to change.

In his ambivalence about wishing to change, a client projects onto his counselor the attributes of significant persons in his past who were helpful as well as the attributes of persons who were hurtful. In the process of assessing, understanding, and reacting to the ambivalence of the client, the counselor's own ambivalence may become activated if he uncritically believes either side of the client's projections. That the counselor becomes ambivalent and is immobilized by a client's projections or fantasies is no accident. The power of the client's projections and the rapidity with which these projections may switch from positive to negative may be very confusing to the counselor. The counselor's confusion may well revolve around his inability to cope with the client's double messages. The counselor may then become ambivalent and wonder, "Am I helpful or am I hurtful?"

When a client is ambivalently struggling to change, he will be very sensitive to the corresponding ambivalence in the counselor's behavior which he can use to immobilize him. How vulnerable the counselor is to becoming immobilized by the client may be a function of a number of the counselor's own concerns. An impasse in their relationship, then, may also arise out of the counselor's own conflicts about his adequacy; it may occur because of the counselor's anxiety about the depths to which he may need to go to help the client, or it may be a consequence of the counselor's being engulfed by the fantasies of the client.

If an impasse is reached because of the counselor's ambivalence, it may be resolved in a number of ways depending on what has activated that ambivalence. Within the relationship we have observed that, although a client may be sensitive to and use the counselor's ambivalence to destroy the relationship, clients will also attempt to preserve the relationship. At times it may become necessary, through supervision or consultation with someone outside the relationship, to help free the counselor. Being freed from his ambivalence on one occasion is not a final solution, however, because the counselor's ability to help is something that must be continually resolved throughout the entire process. The counselor's ambivalence is continually reactivated because he is constantly confronted with new demands on him and with the consequences of his own behavior. The resolution process goes on and counseling is successful insofar as the counselor's ambivalence is continually resolved in a manner that will benefit the client.

UNDERSTANDING—SYMPATHIZING

A more specific way of differentiating between appropriate and in
appropriate counselor responses to the eliciting behaviors of the
client is to consider the counselor's feelings and behaviors along
an understanding-sympathetic dimension. Understanding or em‑
pathic behavior consists of the counselor's adequate responses to the
client's genuine bids for help. These behaviors and feelings are
the ones that are directed toward the goal of changing the client.
When the counselor responds to the eliciting behaviors that have
defensive value to the client as though the feelings associated with
behaviors are the problem feelings, then the counselor is being
sympathetic or identifying with the client instead of being understanding. The consequences of this sympathetic behavior are the
precipitating events which lead to healthy resistance on the part
of the client.

Whereas sympathetic behavior leads to healthy resistance, em-
pathetic behavior may evoke defensive resistance. The budding
signs of defensive resistance in the client create critical incidents
in the counseling relationship since these are the moments in the
process when the client's defenses and conflicts are most likely to
be activated. Since the purpose of a counseling relationship is
to change a person, the counselor needs to continue to believe at
these critical times that his behavior is appropriate. He is likely to
discount his effectiveness if his own conflicts interfere with his
understanding of the meaning of the resistance.

The client, for example, may feel critical of the counselor who
has been understanding and has elicited anxiety. Whether the
counselor becomes immobilized by the client's criticalness is a function of how sensitive he is to the ways in which this particular
person resists. Provided that the counselor understands the client's
reaction as a response to fear related to the counselor's disorganizing his defenses, the counselor may skirt an impasse and minimize
the resistance.

Resistance to help from a counselor is something that almost
always occurs in a client, and the process of counseling is a con-

tinual testing of the counselor's adequacy. Resistance will substantially increase as the client's defenses are weakened, and the basic conflicts begin to rise to the surface. To maintain his defenses, the client will go to great extremes to minimize, criticize, or threaten the counselor in other ways. At these points, the relationship may reach its greatest crises, for the client can make the counselor feel most intensely that he has been in error. Provided that the counselor is continually sensitive to the client's real problems and the meanings of the client's defensive coping behaviors, the client will begin to internalize and modify his usual behaviors.

INTERNALIZATION-EXTERNALIZATION

Clients approaching the counseling relationship often regard their problems as environmental, and they foresee the process of resolving the problem as being that of learning new ways to manipulate their environment. We feel that clients may attempt to structure the counseling relationship in this way to defend against their anxiety about dealing with the problem as an internal one. This client motivation to externalize does not mean that a client cannot be helped to internalize. It does create a problem for the counselor, however, in that the client may devote much energy in attempts to change the counselor or to somehow try to prevent him from helping the client to internalize his feelings.

Even though clients have been unsuccessful in solving their problems by environmental manipulation, many of them still retain a tendency to see their problems as external to themselves. They continue to hope that they can solve their problems by manipulating the environment. When the client enters counseling, he believes, and this is the insatiable cyclical aspect of his behavior, that if he can manipulate or change the counselor as he has attempted to change other persons in his environment, he will solve his problems.

We see a parallel between efforts to change the counselor and continuing persistent efforts to change parents. That is, the client's attempts to change his counselor, we would feel, represent a displaced form of earlier and even continuing current attempts to modify the relationship between the client and his parents. The client wishes to maintain the myth that without internal change he eventually will become potent enough to cause his parents to behave differently toward him.

How the counselor responds to the eliciting behaviors of the client may either help the client to internalize his problem and work on it appropriately or unwittingly permit him to maintain the fantasy that the solution to the problem resides somehow in continuing to manipulate the environment. Through the counseling process, the client may thus learn that his greatest concession is to change himself in order to be able to restructure his environment.

DIAGNOSIS: AN ONGOING INTERPERSONAL PROCESS

According to the arguments that we will present, the behavior of the counselor and client has a continuing effect on both; and it is as a result of the consequences of this interpersonal impact that the therapeutic relationship accrues and change occurs. Diagnosis, in such a theory of change, is an interpersonal process in which the sole purpose of the diagnosis is to understand the relationship well enough to be able to help the client to change. Looked at in this way, assessment becomes a living, changing, exciting process that arises out of the counselor's growing perception as to the cause of his client's problems, what he must experience in order to change, and how the counselor can use himself in this relationship to help the client to make the necessary changes.

Any therapeutic relationship tends to be more distant at the outset, and early diagnosis is necessarily based upon more generic notions of what clients' problems are than on any conception of what a particular client's problems are. When a counselor and a client meet, the counselor picks up a number of cues about the client's problems and casts these cues into a framework of other problems that other people have brought to him that seem to be similar in various ways to this client's problems. But the very nature of the abstracting process means that the counselor and client in this relationship are distant since, in its generic form, the diagnosis reveals little about the source of this client's problems, about what motivated this client to develop these behaviors, or even about what they mean to the client.

The initial diagnosis is only one of the means that the counselor has of setting the counseling relationship into motion. As the counseling process continues to progress appropriately, the process of diagnosis becomes a more intimate, idiosyncratic one. Unless this idiosyncratic development occurs, the lack of specificity in the diagnosis is a reflection of the fact that the participants in this relationship have not caused it to be therapeutic. Whether the counselor's diagnosis changes will be a function of whether the relationship becomes closer, because only in an intimate relationship is it safe for the client to talk about the meaning that his behavior has for him. The counselor demonstrates his ineffectiveness in getting the relationship into motion when he clings to the original conception about his client. Further, such tenacity with regard to the generic diagnosis is a way of defending against the fact that the counselor has effected a poor relationship with his client.

We tend to think of diagnosis and counseling as inseparable processes with varying emphases as the nature and closeness of the relationship changes. When the diagnostic process is maximum in the generic sense, the relationship is minimal. The counselor's increasing understanding of the client's dynamics and the meaning that the client's problems have for him is a function of an intensifying relationship. As the relationship grows stronger, the diagnosis necessarily becomes more specific to this person, and the counselor leaves the generic ideas farther and farther behind him as he and the client delve more deeply into the meanings of his experiences.

SUPERVISION: FREEING THE COUNSELOR

The position that we have taken in this first chapter leads naturally to considering supervision as a vital adjunct to counseling. The process of supervision can be approached in much the same way as the developing interpersonal diagnosis which we have just described. As the supervisory relationship develops, the supervisor becomes an increasingly significant figure in the development of the counselor.

We view supervision as a process in which the supervisor struggles to discover how he can best assist the counselor in establishing adequate and effective relationships with his clients. The supervisory relationship is useful to the counselor if it enables him to view all of himself—needs, conflicts, life experience—as potentially helpful to his clients. Supervision is not, therefore, a process of unraveling and resolving the counselor's conflicts, but rather it is a process of mobilizing his adequacy.

Supervision is neither a didactic process nor is it a therapeutic process. However, the supervisory relationship does have in common with the counseling process some of the qualities of an intense face-to-face relationship. This commonality with the therapeutic endeavor stems from the content and purpose of the supervisory relationship. In supervision, we study the dynamic interaction of the supervisee and his clients in order to assist him in finding ways of being productive in his counseling relationships. Our goal as supervisors, therefore, is to promote individualized, spontaneous, and resourceful behavior rather than to reward emulation.

SUMMARY

This book is concerned with how people present themselves for counseling, how they defend themselves, how they struggle to surrender and yet hold on to their problems, and how they can trick the counselor into helping them to defend against behavior change. The recurring theme is that everything that occurs in the counseling relationship is determined by the previous behavior of one or the other of the two interacting parties. The book is further based on the assumption that the counselor's attitudes toward the client and the client's problems may arouse his own ambivalence about helping the client. Only if the counselor is able to resolve his own ambivalence, can the client state his case and resolve his ambivalence about changing.

A final assumption is that the counselor's attitudes and ambivalences, whatever they may be and however they are stimulated, in turn move the client to act out in the counseling relationship all of the essential elements of his conflicts. Our conclusion is founded on the hope that the counselor will be able in retrospect to utilize the client's behavior to understand how he was instrumental in activating the client's conflicts and how he can use this information in a therapeutic way to help the client to change.

DIMENSIONS
OF A COUNSELING RELATIONSHIP

Chapter 2

The complexities, subtleties, and intensity of a counseling relationship increase dramatically as the relationship becomes more meaningful to the participants. The increasing significance of the relationship is the key to its therapeutic value. But the value of a close relationship is only potentially therapeutic because the intensity of a relationship can at once be its strength and its weakness. The potency of a relationship resides in the commitment and affective involvement of the client and his counselor; but a commitment to change implies vulnerability. The power of a relationship necessary to effect change can also make failure to change an equally significant event and have a lasting influence on both participants. For the client, failure may mean confirmation of previous ineffective interpersonal relationships; for the counselor, it may mean that his next counseling relationship labors under residual burden of proof.

Our purpose in this chapter and in the succeeding chapters is to expand and clarify the dimensions of a therapeutic relationship. At this time, we will concern ourselves with the essential qualities of the relationship, and we will use the following chapters to relate these dimensions to the dynamics and stimulus value of the counselor and client.

Introduction to the Dimensions

The participants of the therapeutic encounter have an increasingly intense and reciprocal impact on each other. We believe that the counselor and client constantly stimulate each other to behave in ways that may either help or hinder the client's changing. Not only does the counselor activate the conflicted feelings in his client, but the client is similarly stimulating counselor conflicts. The relationship that ensues, then, is a function of the dynamics of both parties.

Such a way of formulating the nature of the counseling relationship implies that the behaviors of both participants may be modified by their effects on each other. The counselor may be changed by the relationship even though the intent is to change the client. In a sense, the counselor's changing is incidental to the process; for it is his being aware of what is happening to him in the process that is therapeutic to the client and enables the client to change. In fact, we would propose that a relationship in which the counselor is not affectively involved and is not confronted by his own dynamics and conflicts with possible consequent changes in his own behavior may not be a therapeutic encounter for the client.

The course of a developing counseling relationship is one in which the counselor's stimulus value triggers response patterns in the client, which, in turn, have an impact on the counselor. The reciprocal impact of these responses is effecting behavioral responses in the participants at a number of levels. At one level of communication the client's responses will be specifically directed to the counselor's actual questions and statements: the contentual matter of the relationship. In addition, the counselor's stimulation will trigger a number of associational processes in the client that are a function of his general life experiences that he has brought into the relationship. Later in this chapter we will elaborate on how the levels of communication occur in the relationship.

As the client continues to relate to his counselor, his responses are increasingly governed by and specifically related to this particular relationship. In this respect the client's projections, associations, and feelings about this relationship assume more and more reality with regard to this relationship as well as having increasing meaning to him in terms of past experiences in his own life. What this means is that as counseling progresses, the demands on the counselor will become increasingly intense as these demands become more and more a function of and a consequence of the counselor's impact on the client and his own stimulation of the client. The counselor, in other words, is increasingly confronted by the consequences of his own behavior. How this concept can be at once threatening and relieving and how it can be useful is pointed out later in this chapter.

Consequences of the developing relationship also manifest themselves in the client. Under the stress of the relationship, he may retreat to his most useful defenses or somehow attempt to reduce the effectiveness of the counselor. The stalemating of a relationship, therefore, can be a consequence of the behavior of either participant. In the next chapters, we will elaborate on how a relationship can be impeded with regard to the eliciting behaviors, the concepts of the resistances, and the needs of the client and counselor.

Provided that the counselor and client negotiate a relationship and that the counselor meets the threat of being confronted with the consequences of his own behavior, the relationship will develop and the client's associational process will continue to expand as he is increasingly stimulated in the interviews. As the circle of the client's feeling states becomes increasingly expansive, the sequence of events in the relationship will become increasingly related both to the client's associational process as it relates to his past behavior and as a reflection of the current counseling relationship.

How the sequence of events mirrors the relationship, how the content reflects the relationship, and how both of these concepts are important to the course of the client's conflicted behavior is explained in this chapter. As the relationship develops, the content of the client's associational process and the meaning the client attributes to events that occur in the counseling hour and between sessions will be a reflection of the relationship. The sequential events of association and attribution can be very useful to the progress of counseling provided that the counselor utilizes the information just as he utilizes the actual content of the associational process.

Reciprocal Impact of Client and Counselor

When a client and counselor enter a relationship, both participants introduce into that relationship their total life experiences. The counselor enters this relationship with many attitudes that stem from different aspects of his experiences. In one respect, the counselor's attitudes are a product of his professional experiences and training. From the counselor's training, he enters the relationship with an orientation toward this particular client which is a function of a number of generic ideas about how people develop, how problems get started, how problems are manifested, and how conflicts can be resolved. In another way, the counselor views the client and his problems from his own dynamics and conflicts. These experiential aspects of the counselor are inevitably a part of the relationship, and, provided the counselor is constantly aware of their influence in the relationship, he can utilize his own dynamics in a therapeutic way with his client. The counselor, then, functions more or less effectively as a consequence of his professional training and experience; yet his own experiential person is constantly intertwined in the counseling process and facilitates or impedes as the case may be.

The client brings to the counseling relationship his own conflicts which have arisen out of frustrations in his previous interactions with other people. From these conflicts with others he has developed generalized attitudes about people and whether they can be helpful. From his experiences with people, from what he has read, and even from previous encounters with other counselors, the client enters the relationship with some ideas about what counselors are like, what he wishes to keep secret, what he wishes to change, and perhaps even some ideas about how this change should take place.

The question, therefore, is not one of whether the participants in the relationship enter it with any preconceived ideas about counseling. The expectations of both parties serve as the substratum on which the relationship will be built. The question is one of how immediately helpful the counselor's and client's combined attitudes will be for the relationship, and either person's beliefs may have to be modified in the process. When the counselor's and client's expectations are in conflict, there must be a period of negotiating. The client may not be the only one to make concessions in order to initiate the relationship; the counselor may need to concede some things in order to activate the relationship. These counselor concessions will be appropriate if they are based on the client's healthy demands—his needs rather than his wants.

The concessions that the counselor makes should ideally be made in terms of a thorough understanding of his client's dynamics. But such an ideal situation is not possible from the generic kinds of information that a counselor has early in the relationship; so it is particularly easy at early points in the relationship for the counselor to err in judgment. The probability of erring here may immobilize the counselor because he knows that the consequences of the error will be expressed immediately or later on in the relationship. However, if the counselor can recognize the consequences of his own behavior and not view error as irrevocable, then he can freely react to the client and still assist in rendering the corrective experiences as they accrue in the relationship.

No matter what transpires between the participants of the relationship, the consequences of the behaviors are potentially useful for developing a successful relationship. If the client introduces material into the relationship which reflects a negative attitude on his part toward the counselor and their relationship, the course of future counseling will be determined by how effectively the counselor can come to grips with the dynamic meaning of the client's message. When the client reports, for example, that he is upset by feelings that the counselor has aroused in him, the counselor's response is a function of how threatened he is by the confrontation. If the counselor's competence is threatened, he may react by feeling guilty, overwhelmed, and impotent and may consequently do nothing to further the relationship. A second counselor may become aggressive, hostile, and dogmatic in an effort to restore his potency by activity. Both counselors labor under the same irrational premise that the client can somehow control their potency.

In each case the counselors' responses are governed by their own needs and conflicts rather than from an evaluation of what the client's behavior means. More appropriate counselor behavior will result if the counselor is dynamically free enough to listen to what the client says and can think in terms of what he has done to stimulate this kind of response in the client. In discovering the sequence of events that activated the client's responses, the counselor may acquire some insight into what the client's conflicts are and how they are mobilized. Knowing this about the client and remembering that his task is to change the client, the counselor may then be able to evaluate more adequately the meaning and appropriateness of the client's disturbance.

Miss Nora—Demonstrating the Reciprocal Impact

We think of Miss Nora as presenting a common kind of problem that reflects the reciprocal impact of the counselor's and client's interchange. When Miss Nora met with her male counselor for the first time, she communicated very quickly that she was a difficult person to know and to like and that few males had successfully related to her. She indicated, however, that she had received some help from the intake counselor and that she felt grateful to him. The impact of her initial communication—that she was hard to know and like but that she had found a male whom she could respond to —may affect a counselor in a number of ways. A counselor may feel challenged by her and competitive with her previous counselor. At another level the impact of the challenge may be experienced as a threat to a counselor's competence, and, if the threat is experienced intensely, the counselor may not be able to feel the strength of the client's wish for help and her capacity to relate.

With these few statements, Miss Nora set the developing relationship into motion by revealing significant information about how she meets, interacts, and copes with males; and the counselor's potential response to the client's initial confrontation will activate the relationship. The client's statements are probably compacted packages of the ways in which she has learned to relate to significant persons in her past. Although such guesses are too tentative to be useful immediately in the sense that the counselor may make immediate verbal or behavioral responses to them, the information can be held in abeyance for later encounters. We propose that early statements such as these may eventually emerge as significant features in the development and manifestation of the client's problems.

These early compacted statements of the client are the means by which the counselor begins to help the client to understand, explore, and expand his feelings. The process in which the counselor uses these initial compact statements to assist the client to expand his feelings is the way that we feel the diagnostic process is interpersonally implemented in a relationship. The counselor has a number of alternatives open to him, and his response to the client will reflect how he has experienced the impact of the client's statements. Some of the alternatives available to the counselor are more therapeutically helpful to the client than others, but whatever alternative the counselor chooses and for whatever emotional and professional reasons he does so, the impact of his response in the client can be corrected and even his errors can be therapeutically productive. Provided that the counselor is able to cope with the consequences of his behavior and its effect on the client, either immediately or through supervision, the behavior can be incorporated productively into the counseling relationship.

Miss Nora's counselor actually did respond by feeling challenged. That is, her counselor behaved defensively by indicating to his client that he had reviewed her case with the intake counselor and that he liked her and wanted her to trust him as she had the other counselor. The counselor's verbal response to the client was a twofold expression of his internal response which was characterized by feelings of competitiveness and self-deprecation. We would tend to consider this response as initially, but again not irrevocably, nonproductive of changing the client for several reasons. The counselor's needs took precedence over hearing the client's statements as reflecting her problem and need. He also placed himself in a competitive and manipulative marketplace in the same way as other significant persons had done in her past. In addition, his response revealed much of his dynamics and vulnerability to the client.

Since the counselor's dynamics entered into the relationship so soon and so intensely, we might infer that his client had struck a resonant chord close to the counselor's own conflicts. When this "error" is viewed from the intensity of the dynamics involved, it would seem to be a more difficult error to correct without recourse to supervision. But again, the counselor's vulnerability is the very thing that can eventually have a therapeutic effect on the client for it indicates that the counselor can be affected by the client, and as long as he is aware of how he becomes affected, he can help the client.

Whatever response the counselor "felt" as a consequence of the impact of the client's opening remarks, he might have established a more productive relationship with her had he maintained his response internally, been open-ended in questioning what it was she meant by her statement, or perhaps simply reserved the information for future use. We are inclined to think that the reciprocal nature of the relationship is better facilitated, at least in the early stages of the relationship, if the client reveals herself first, a reversal of events that occurred in this case. We believe that the more veiled the counselor is during these early encounters, the more opportunity there is for the client to expand his own feelings and attitudes and to present those aspects of himself that he feels are significant to the problem.

When we speak of the counselor as being veiled we are referring to the counselor's veiling his intentions and meanings. We do not equate veiling with inactivity, however, for the counselor may be quite active even though his intent may be concealed or unclear to the client. This ambiguity or veiling by the counselor provides the client with the opportunity to make the counselor into the particular kind of significant figure the client needs the counselor to be. In addition, the counselor can selectively reveal those aspects of himself later when he knows the meaning they have to this client's change and growth.

Without knowing what the impact of his response that he "liked" Miss Nora meant to her, the counselor could not predict what effects this would have upon their relationship, and he would necessarily have difficulty in understanding the client's responses. In this particular case, when the counselor expressed a liking for her, Miss Nora questioned whether she was ready to be liked by the counselor and indicated that she was easily able to "see through" people and felt frightened by her ability to do so. It may be, for example, that this same sequence of events had happened to Miss Nora in her past since she seems to need to activate men to compete for her affection.

Provided that the counselor had been free enough to listen to the client, he could have understood better what the consequences of being "liked" inappropriately meant to the client. These feelings were somehow associated with her apparent fears of becoming omnipotent or controlling and manipulating men. In addition, the client was apparently attempting to activate the counselor to behave appropriately with her. The counselor might internalize this information too, because it is indicative of the fact that the client sees herself as a source of strength and control and is ambivalent about having such power over men.

Even in these few exchanges, the reciprocal impact of the counselor and client is felt and the course of the relationship has begun to develop. The consequences of the counselor's current behavior will be felt throughout their relationship, and he will be constantly confronted by what he is now stimulating in the client. If the counselor becomes so emotionally responsive that he cannot evaluate his stimulus value, the relationship may reach an impasse quite quickly as evidenced by increasing circularity in content, affect, and associational processes. On the other hand, if the counselor becomes aware of his own conflicted feelings, as actually happened in this case, the relationship will mature.

Creating Relationships

As a result of the counselor's own dynamics and conflicts, he may be able to create relationships with varying degrees of freedom in which his clients can express and explore their conflicts. Whether the counselor will be able to create a wide range of healthy relationships depends on how free he is to respond to a wide repertoire of the client's eliciting behaviors and how willing he is to engage in relationships of many different varieties. We are talking about a continuum of variations in counselor willingness and ability to participate in the resolution of a variety of client problems. We think of the therapeutic ideal as the counselor who is able to help the client to achieve a controlled expansiveness of the client's feelings, associations, and conflicts.

A counselor's conflicts and dynamics may also make it necessary for him to inhibit the client so that he experiences and expresses very limited and invariant behaviors. Counselors may tend to inhibit their clients for different reasons. One type of inhibiting behavior may develop in which the counselor becomes conflicted because he finds the affective intensity of the relationship a frightening experience. A second type of inhibiting behavior by a counselor may arise out of his own fantasies about the projected intensity of the relationship in the future. Both of these types of internal behavioral responses may lead to apparently similar counselor behaviors, but we feel that the counselor feelings which motivate the different inhibiting behaviors are quite different. In both cases, the counselor may resort to premature interpretations of the client's behavior as a defense against experiencing affect. Both counselors may resort to controlling the client's responses and to leading him into areas that will not expose the counselor's conflicts.

Even though the actual counselor behaviors in the interviews may be similar, the effects on the client may be quite different. We believe this difference stems from the fact that the motivations arise from different internal conflicts and from the temporal difference in the activation and expression of the counselor's inhibiting defenses in the relationship. If the counselor's need to inhibit arises out of the actual affective intensity of the relationship, his need has arisen out of the consequences of some real human encounters. The effects of this kind of interaction for the client are potentially heathier than those in which the counselor inhibits in anticipation that he and the client will reach this level of affective intensity.

In order for a relationship to have matured to the point of affective intensity, the counselor may well have demonstrated potency in the relationship, and, through supervision or some other method of consultation, he may be able to reestablish his adequacy. In the case of Miss Nora, the counselor's initial responses to the client may precipitate an impasse where failure can be significant to the client, and the counselor as well, if the counselor is unable to reestablish the relationship. The counselor's actual responses to Miss Nora, although possibly inappropriate, were nevertheless active attempts on his part to have an intense affective encounter. The rewards for successfully working through the difficulty can be monumental for both participants.

If, on the other hand, the counselor were to inhibit the client because of his anticipatory fears and projections about the consequences of a fantasied, intense relationship, the client will not even have the opportunity to state his case. Since a relationship has never developed, the client will not experience this encounter as a significant interpersonal failure. In this case, the experience of personal failure is avoided by both participants; but since nothing was risked, nothing was gained. This kind of limited risk-taking by the counselor is indicative of a counselor for whom supervision may not be productive.

But relationships are reciprocal and the client may present himself in such a way that he intends for the counselor to feel that there are limited ways in which the counselor can be helpful. In this way, the limiting agent may be the client rather than the counselor; but such attempts to control or limit the counselor's effectiveness are in the nature of the therapeutic encounter and are amenable to change. The affect and behavior of the client may be powerfully convincing to the counselor however, and the counselor's behavioral repertoire may become truncated and ineffective if he believes that the client must be treated very carefully for some reason. For example, a client may attempt to convince the counselor that he must attenuate his response pattern because the client suggests through his affect and behaviors that unless he is treated in a particular way he will possibly leave counseling or behave in uncontrolled ways.

If, verbally and behaviorally, the client successfully communicates his threatening message, whatever its content or meaning may be, the counselor's ability to respond freely to the cues he gets from the client about problem areas may be seriously damaged. Once the counselor believes that the client can not tolerate the necessary anxiety or is not resilient enough to incorporate the impact of exploration, the counselor will be immobilized. What the counselor may be failing to see is that the client has manipulated the situation in precisely this way so as to maintain the myth that his problems are too complex for anyone to be of help to him.

Under stress, a client will be very sensitive to the feelings of others, including the counselor, and may attempt to utilize this sensitivity to keep his problems intact rather than to change. A specific way in which a client may attempt to avoid changing is to try to ward off the counselor by searching for content that has conflicted meaning for the counselor. Even when the client reacts to something in the counselor that is a real conflict for him, the counselor needs to continue to assume that the client's conflicted feelings are independent of his own conflicts and that the client is focusing on the counselor for his own defensive purposes. By refocusing on the client's motivation, the counselor may avoid an impasse. Otherwise the counselor may become introspective and believe that he must change in order for the client to change. The counselor should remember that his purpose is to change the client and that, although he has problems, the client is picking away at these counselor conflicts for good reasons of his own.

Here again, if the counselor begins to believe that his value to the client is more than a stimulus value for the client's associational process, he will think that he must be invulnerable before he can help the client. Although the counselor must be aware of his vulnerability so that he can utilize that information in the process of working with a client, he need not have his own problems resolved in order to help his client change.

As the counseling relationship continues to develop, the intensity of the relationship grows. The internal demands on the counselor also increase as he recognizes that he is responsible for the ensuing relationship and for the behavioral consequences of whatever he stimulates in the client. Pacing the client's anxiety and associational patterns so that they produce change is a difficult and anxiety-provoking task. The counselor may feel progressively immobilized especially as the client feeds back into the relationship his increasing anxiety and begins to relate his anxiety more and more to this particular relationship and to this counselor.

We have noted, however, that there is an associative link between a counselor's becoming immobilized by a client's demands and his acceptance of inappropriate responsibility. What the counselor may need to remember, and perhaps take comfort in, is the thought that, although he has a responsibility to assist the client in the resolution of his conflicts and is the stimulus for the expression of the conflicts in this relationship, he is not the causative agent for the generic conflict. He needs to be constantly aware of the fact that as the agent in the relationship it is he who activates and intensifies the generic conflicts and who stimulates their expression, but that he is not the source of the conflict. If the counselor does take the responsibility for the generic conflict, then he is making the error of omnipotence.

The intensity of the client's confrontation that he is anxious and experiencing internal pressures and the counselor's own awareness of the powerful effect that he is having on the client's feelings of disorganization may activate some concern in the counselor about his own omnipotence. Actually, the intensity of the client's confrontation is often a validation of the fact that the counselor has been effective in the relationship. But the power of the relationship may activate enough counselor conflict so that the counselor may attempt to undo what he has achieved because he cannot tolerate these feelings. His anxiety may lead him to attempt to reduce his effectiveness by changing or breaking up the client's associational process, by directing the course of conversation toward himself, or by other maneuvers. When the counselor resorts to such egocentric behavior, he may then have shifted his position from one of accepting appropriate responsibility to one of acquiescing to his own conflicted feelings and to the client's demands without regard for the therapeutic value of his behavior.

We return again to the idea that the counselor's task is to help the client to express his problems. In order to provide a situation in which a client can recall and work out conflicted feelings, the counselor must provide the emotional strength and security for the client to do so. And, as we said earlier, it is in fact only because the counselor has been successful in achieving this goal that feelings of omnipotence may have entered the picture. In this respect, we are suggesting that there is a dynamic relationship between the concepts of strength and omnipotence.

When the client experiences the counselor's strength, then the intensity of the relationship grows, and the client begins to attribute earlier conflicts to the counselor and to lean heavily on him. The counselor's strength has invited the expression of the client's needs; even so, when the counselor experiences the intensity of the client's demands, he may experience equally powerful anxiety of his own. His anxiety at such times may stem from a number of sources. Mixed fears and wishes about omnipotence is just one example of a source of anxiety. Other feelings will intrude and may tend to deactivate a relationship.

When a client comes to rely upon a counselor for support to explore his conflicted feelings, the counselor may confuse his therapeutic responsibility with feelings about his adequacy to be the client's father or mother. Here again, we would feel that the "weight" of the feelings are directly proportional to the amount of inappropriate responsibility that the counselor shoulders. Inevitably, when the counselor inappropriately assumes that he must be the parent that the client never had, he will simultaneously arouse in himself feelings of omnipotence and inadequacy. Once the counselor can accept the counseling relationship on the grounds that he cannot be the parent of the client, he will be freed to be the best substitute that the client could have. If the counselor is clear about the relationship, he will not be threatened by the client's accusations that he is a professional person and doesn't care about the client. He will be able to respond by agreeing that he may be a substitute but that he wants to help the client. And the therapeutic venture is one of providing a good enough substitute to allow the client to undergo as an adult those experiences which were too frightening for him to confront as a child.

When the relationship reaches the intensity we are suggesting here, the client is most vulnerable; for the intensity reflects the significance of the relationship. Whether change occurs in the client is a function of how well the participants surmount the critical incidents that arise when the relationship has reached this level. The problem at these crucial moments in counseling is not one of error. The basic premise of this book is that errors are inevitable but revocable and that relationships are resilient. But at those decisive times where the counseling relationship is intense and the client's confrontation reaches into the depths of his conflicts, we have noted not only that a client's conflicts are most active and clear, but that the conflicts are experienced and expressed in a compressed way. The issue of error then becomes one of how rapidly the counselor can recover and be of assistance therapeutically.

Miss Edna—Activating a Counselor's Conflicts

The interplay of many of the characteristics that we have been describing are reflected in the counseling relationship that developed between Miss Edna and her male counselor. The particular problems that Miss Edna brought to that relationship and the way that she defended against a mature relationship are not important to our discussion here. We would like to describe what happened when the relationship became intense and when the counselor became frightened by the intensity of the affective involvement.

Consistently throughout the developing relationship, the counselor behaved with strength and warmth, two characteristics that the client found confusing in the same person. The counselor's behavior had its desired effect, and the client began to experience anxiety and associated it to earlier experiences that were at the source of her fears. The critical incident occurred when, under the stress of anxiety, the client began to criticize the counselor for the disorganized way she was feeling and to contend that this relationship was responsible for all of her current interpersonal troubles.

Rather than to evaluate the meaning of the client's affect and statements in terms of the client's proximity to experiencing change, the counselor's own anxiety about the power of the feelings that he had stimulated and his own fears about the weight of the client's dependency overwhelmed him; and he responded by being behaviorally apologetic for the client's state. The consequence of the emotional insecurity generated in the client by the wavering counselor's behavior had a marked effect on the interview. The client's previously manifested interpersonal defenses were reactivated and, in a tightly compressed way, the client reenacted the entire cycle of her conflicts during the next few minutes of the counseling hour.

In our discussion with her counselor, he indicated that the sudden change in his client's interview behavior was startling enough to him so that he recognized the reenactment of her conflicts as associated to something that he had triggered. The therapeutic value of the error in this case was dramatically turned into productive use because the counselor called his client's attention to what had actually occurred between them. In this way, the counselor's admission of error was a show of strength and the ensuing exploration of how it had come about at once rejuvenated his strength and revitalized the client's feelings about him.

THE COMPACTED PICTURE: EXPANDING
THE FEELINGS

Earlier we alluded to the fact that very early in their therapeutic encounters clients present a compact picture of the genesis, development, and interpersonal manifestations of their conflicts. This picture which the client presents is a synthesis of his whole life history expressed in terms of the significant content of his life. The client has compressed many experiences into a few ways of thinking about himself. The corollary to this compacted content is that there will have been affect associated with each of these past experiences which has been similarly compressed. Accompanying the compacted content there is, then, compacted affect out of the past.

The compacted experiences of the client serve many functions for him. The client has compressed his experiences for good reasons and one of these is that in its present form, the affect, although anxiety provoking, is not as painful as it would be if it were expanded. The anxiety is more dormant and encysted. If the experience is expanded, the fear of the client is that it will flow into all aspects of his life and become overwhelming. But the fear of being overwhelmed is countered with a fear of continuing to live with the anxiety which he does experience.

A counselor has several courses open to him when the compacted picture is presented to him. He may take the compacted experience that is presented to him and search through it, looking for specifics in content that he can feed back to the client so that the client will elaborate on those particular experiences. If, for example, the client presents information about his attitude toward parents and siblings, the counselor might ask the client to elaborate on what the relationship with a sibling may have been like. Another way that a counselor may respond to the client's compacted experience is to cast the information into the framework of some generic diagnostic category that he may be able to utilize to begin understanding the client.

In our listening to therapeutic interviews, we have found a more useful approach to these compacted experiences. In order to activate a dynamic counseling relationship, we suggest that the counselor search for the recurring affective theme that pervades the material. As the client presents these compacted affective and contentual experiences, the counselor can often abstract from the various experiences an understanding of some basic affect. The way in which the person views himself that is carried thematically throughout the presenting content generally refers to a very basic attitude that the person has toward himself. In these cases the counselor may abstract first the most general experience of affect that is characteristic of all of the experiences that the client is attempting to relate, such as noting that the client views himself as being a "bad" person or an "overburdened" person.

If the counselor can effectively perceive and respond in this way, he has tuned in at the most general level possible to the dynamic meaning of the client's previous experiences. The client then has the most freedom possible to expand his experiences and feelings in the ways that have the most significance to him. As the client begins to expand the associated feelings, the counselor can follow the course of the client's conflicts. By following the client's lead as to which experiences have the most meaning for him, the counselor can more effectively track the development of the client's conflicts. Also by responding thus, the counselor has been genuinely supportive and effective, and yet by so responding he remains appropriately veiled.

Miss Joanne—Expanding the Compacted Experiences

An example of how a counselor derived a basic affective theme from the compacted experiences of a client occurred in the case of Miss Joanne. In their first interview, Miss Joanne presented a great deal of information about her current and past conflicts. She talked of her academic difficulties and childhood experiences with her

parents and siblings and how they had ignored her. Throughout
the entire presentation, the counselor noted a basic theme pervad-
ing the content which we have noted to be reminiscent of many
highly conflicted persons. The affect undergirding the theme was
that the client viewed her problems as being very complex and that
she did not consider any of her past relationships satisfying in the
sense that anyone had taken the time to understand her.

The counselor captured the affective undertones of this recurring theme at a critical moment in the interview by saying, "I
guess that you think your problems are pretty complicated and that
people tend to belittle them and really don't understand you. Is
that right?" Such a response as the foregoing, if it accurately reflects the basic theme, has the effect of freeing the client to begin
the process of elaborating the compacted picture.

Had the counselor approached the client's presentation by suggesting or insisting that the client elaborate one of the experiences,
the course of that relationship would have been somewhat altered.
Such a counselor posture in regard to specifics must have a defi-
nite impact on the client's expectations regarding the nature of
the ensuing relationship. The impact of the communication is that
the counselor's opinions about the significance of events are more
important than the client's own experiencing of critical events. Such
an attempted direction could possibly jeopardize a relationship in
its early stages because the counselor has no way of knowing what
his intervention means to the client. To expand this notion, we have
noted that male clients sometimes enter a counseling relationship
with many fears of being dominated and controlled. When the
counselor attempts to direct the counseling session toward specifics
as we have described above, he may confirm the client's expectations about male relationships as consisting of control and subjuga-
tion before the relationship is strong enough to support the exploration and resolution of such conflicts.

Although the actual content of the early encounters may be
important information that the counselor stores and may use later
to facilitate change, his understanding and utilization of the basic
affective theme that undergirds many of the client's experiences
should often be the essential component for activating a therapeutic relationship. The ensuing counseling relationship expands

and clarifies the meaning of the theme. In the course of exploring and elaborating the compressed affect underlying the general theme, much of the actual content of the early relationship may be reintroduced. But the reintroduction of this information is then effected as a dynamic consequence of the reactivated emotional conflicts of the client.

In the case of Miss Joanne who thought that her problems were complicated and that people did not take the time to understand her, the counselor's initial recognition of these general feelings about herself was intended only to strike a dynamic chord in the client so that she would feel that this might be someone who was different. Also, although the counselor felt that this pervasive theme was in part a screen to keep people from getting close enough to her to find out what her real problems were, his response to her feeling and his use of the current general attitude served to activate the relationship and permitted them to discover and expand the associated fears of people.

We wish to distinguish between accurate sensitive touching on a theme to stimulate the client to expand his feelings and explore his conflicts, and the sympathetic assumption that conscious conflicts are an accurate representation of the deeper struggle. One way of regarding the basic theme is to think of it as the entrée into counseling. The job which remains to be done after the basic theme has been touched upon is to assist the client to develop an understanding of the basic underlying conflicts which have led him to experience himself as a person in this way. The process of counseling then will be one of enlarging and differentiating the affects associated with these experiences so that the client's inner world becomes differentiated enough for him to change.

We wish also to point out that the way in which we have presented this aspect of the counseling experience reflects our earlier allusion to the diagnostic process being an interpersonal one that is constantly interwoven into the relationship and grows as the relationship grows rather than existing as a distinct process. When the counselor accurately responds to the affective undertones of the client's contentual matter, he is being a diagnostician in the best sense since his diagnosis is a product of the basic meanings of events for this particular client.

Such an exploration leads to a dynamic diagnosis and incidentally a difficult one because it implies a total commitment on his part to permit the client to explore those areas of his life that are critical to him. When a counselor responds to such a generic feeling as he did in the case of Miss Joanne, he has opened the door for the client to choose any one of her experiences and to begin to elaborate on her feelings, which could pose a possible consequent threat to both of them. For the counselor, the threat stems from the fact that he will be confronted by the consequences of whatever aspect of the affect the client explores. For the client, the threat may stem from the fact that the counselor has effectively facilitated a deeper exploration of the client's world rather than directing the exploration to surface specifics.

LEVELS OF COMMUNICATION

The client risks expanding some of the feelings associated with his compacted experiences as the counseling relationship matures and becomes more and more significant to him. The client's willingness to risk the anxiety of expanding these experiences is in part a function of how effectively the counselor has touched on the general affective theme of the client's compacted experiences.

As the client's past conflicts are expressed and felt in the present, he becomes genuinely confused about himself. In some ways he is justified in attributing his confusion and increased anxiety to the counseling relationship since the process of counseling is one in which the counselor helps the client to change his current behavior through an intricate weaving back and forth between past experiences and current conflicts. This process of dipping into the past to activate and modify the sources of the client's current concerns complicates the communication process. In other words, the communication expands in both directions—the past and the present— at the same time. As the client's feelings about the meaning of past events become more intense, his feelings about his present relationships, including the counseling relationship, are intensified.

When the client continues to associate to past experiences, and as his feelings about these experiences expand and merge with his present conflicts, he begins increasingly to transfer these feelings to the counselor. New dimensions are added to the communication process as the client begins to feel about his counselor as he has about significant persons in his past. He may begin to conduct himself with the counselor as he either did behave or wanted to behave with these other persons and may attempt to elicit feelings from his counselor that he was unable to evoke in others.

In the counseling relationship the client may "act out" some of his previously frustrated wishes. At the same time that he is attempting to elicit help from the counselor, he may also disparage the counselor's abilities to help because significant persons in his past were seen and felt as ineffective. The intricate interplay of the past and present and the ambivalent feelings that the client experiences toward the counselor, particularly as the counselor takes on many shapes to fill many needs, undergird the communication process.

The Content: mirroring the relationship

A client under stress may communicate different messages to the counselor simultaneously. When the relationship becomes intense, we have noted that the client chooses events out of his past and symbolically presents them to the counselor as a means of communicating to him some of the feelings that he is having about the current relationship and some of his doubts about the counselor's adequacy to meet any of his needs. While at one level the client may communicate to the counselor his faith and confidence in the counselor's ability to satisfy all his needs, at another level he may also communicate fears, concerns, and doubts about this. A client may assure a counselor, for example, that he is succeeding in helping him; but at the same time the client may talk about how weak his father is. We believe that at such times, the counselor should consider the probability that the client is also concerned about the counselor's weakness. The probability of a relationship between the client's expressions and his feelings about the counselor's weakness is strengthened if the client continues to be preoccupied with "weakness."

When the client begins to speak in these metaphorical or symbolic ways about experiences which seem, to the counselor, to be related to their relationship, the counselor may find it necessary to expose the underlying implications to render the experiences more meaningful to the current counseling relationship. The dynamic criterion for the counselor response is to release the client so that he can continue to associate to the feelings that are related to the basic conflict. If, for example, a client repeatedly expresses critical feelings toward others, then for dynamic reasons the counselor may suggest that "Perhaps you feel critical of me." The dynamic underlying the counselor response is that he is not fearful of the client's critical, hostile feelings and that he is perceptive but not punishing.

Counselor adequacy, then, is a function of the ability to recognize and respond directly to feelings, no matter what the feelings are. Lack of response to feelings that are close to the surface and are significant to further exploration leads to continued fear, restlessness, and thoughts of terminating the relationship. The counselor's skill is to reserve his response for those moments when the intensity of the fear or wish is so strong in the client that the effect of recognition will be relieving to the client, strengthen his commitment, and free him to continue associating.

Another example of how the content may be symptomatic of the relationship occurred in a case where change in both verbal and other behavioral content reflected the relationship. In this particular case the client entered the interview with a great deal of affect and the counselor seemed frightened by it. In the next few minutes of the interview, the client changed dramatically from being highly expressive of affect to being constricted and talking in a muted whisper. It was as if she were unable to talk about her problems because they were so frightening to the counselor and consequently to herself that she had to whisper.

When a counselor listens to a client's communication as a behavioral guideline for how a counseling relationship is proceeding, then whatever the client reports of his current life experiences may have some particular relevance to the course of that relationship. To illustrate our point, Mr. Tom and his counselor had been having a good deal of difficulty in communicating effectively with each other. During the course of their difficulties, Mr. Tom approached one of their counseling sessions by reporting difficulties he had been having in getting along with people during the week. He spoke at some length about people being bothersome, irritable, and superficial. The counselor, instead of responding to the dynamic connection between these events as displaced feelings about the adequacy of their present relationship, talked with Mr. Tom as though these incidents were unrelated to their sessions. We suspect that the counselor in this relationship did not respond because he was already feeling guilty and angry about being ineffective. Had the counselor's own mixed feelings about the client not immobilized him, he could have revitalized the relationship by incorporating the client's experience into their interaction.

The Sequence of Events—The Temporal Dimension

Thus far, we have discussed ways in which the content of any particular phase of the ongoing counseling process mirrors the relationship and can be abstracted from the process and studied to determine the effectiveness of that relationship. It would follow from this way of conceptualizing the content as having valuable reflective qualities that the value of this type of formulation is enhanced even more if the sequence of the content is studied as a reflection of the process itself.

We have noted in listening to therapeutic interviews that the sequence of events in the relationship is a manifestation of the client's past conflicts expressed in the current relationship. This formulation implies that the sequential content of the current relationship is a reflection of that relationship as it has developed. It further assumes that the sequential events in the current relationship are a parallel to the development of the client's generic conflicts. This parallel may not be readily apparent; but at times when an impasse is reached, the concept we have been outlining can be useful in tracking the possible associations we have suggested.

In a sense, the content can be studied in "snapshot" fashion as a reflection of the status of the relationship at a given time. But the counselor's motivation for studying the content may be that of trying to understand how the course of this particular relationship is an expression of the course of the client's conflicts and how their current interaction is a reflection of a developmental impasse with regard to the generic conflict. In the latter instance, the counselor focuses on studying the sequence of events as a current projection of the temporal, shifting, and changing quality of the client's conflicts.

One way to illustrate these concepts is to discuss their usefulness at points where the relationship may not be developing. The counselor may attempt at such a time to understand the difficulty by examining very recent content. In this way, he examines the content at this point in time as being a mirror of his relationship with the client. This kind of study may be sufficient to resolve the difficulty and enable the relationship to move ahead. For example, the counselor may note that the client is often talking about being punished and the counselor may search for instances in which his responses might have been perceived as admonitions. Knowing about the client's concern and seeing what activates the concern in their interaction will usually be helpful.

In another instance, a sudden change in the nature of the relationship may be sufficiently complex or significant so that the counselor may need to extend his study beyond that of a particular interview or section of an interview. The significance of the critical interaction may be and probably is a consequence of an entire sequence of events in the developing relationship. The counselor and client in their interaction have probably already recapitulated the entire course of the client's conflict, and the course and quality of their interactions in the counseling relationship have most likely been paralleling the development of the client's conflict. In such a case, where extended interactions have taken place, the counselor may profit from studying an extensive portion of his affective involvement with the client to understand its meaning.

Mr. Evan—Utilizing the Sequence of Events

In the following example, we will demonstrate how a counselor has effectively used the content of an interaction to study the relationship. In addition, he has made good use of a critical incident in an intense relationship to study the sequence of events in that relationship as a reflection of a developmental crisis in the client. The case

of Mr. Evan will assist us here in understanding the ideas that we
have been propounding.

In their initial relationship, Mr. Evan found his counselor to be
an adequate and helpful person. He had made considerable progress until he reached a critical point where he began to experience
the fears that apparently were derived from his own relationship
to his father. Apparently, his father had been adequate for a considerable period of time during Mr. Evan's earlier years, and then,
in the client's adolescence, his father had been unable to cope with
the client's feelings and behavior. At the point in the counseling
relationship where the client began to associate to this kind of material, his affect and the verbal content expressed became circular
and he became increasingly concerned about himself. He became
highly self-critical and spoke of himself as someone who was hopeless and could not be helped.

The counselor's initial reaction to this material was to take it in
a somewhat personal sense, to feel inadequate, and to believe for a
time that he had made some serious therapeutic errors. However, as
the counselor began ruminating about his relationship with this
particular client, he remembered feeling adequate up to this point.
By studying the sequence of events as they had occurred in the relationship he began to understand that the client's fears, although
related to this counselor, were vestiges of fears that this relationship
would fail as earlier ones had failed.

When the counselor recognized this sequence clearly, he was
able to say to the client, "Well, it seems that we have reached a critical point here and that you are beginning to feel that I will fail you
as perhaps your father once did." This remark, although provoking
considerable anxiety, was a sufficient show of counselor strength to
allow the client to continue. The circularity of content and the affective impasse, which was frightening to both client and counselor,
disappeared quickly, and the client proceeded to explore his problems further.

This case exemplifies both aspects of the levels of communication that we have been presenting. The circularity in the affect and
content that the client was experiencing and expressing was a mirror
of the impasse in the relationship. When the counselor noted the
impasse and reviewed his own feelings in the relationship, he was

able to see that the changes in his own affective involvement with the client were similar to the kinds of changes in affective relationships that the client had experienced with his father in his own past.

This critical incident in the counseling process was dynamically determined by a number of relationship phenomena. The progress of counseling had really paralleled the course of significant events and affective experiences of the client to the point of impasse. The relationship was a model of the client's previous significant interactions, and the counselor had been affectively involved enough in the client's experience to reconstruct those relationships.

The behaviors of the participants in this relationship reflect our earlier statements about the likely inevitability of feelings of error as an antecedent to therapeutic change. We could view the counselor's preoccupation with his own feelings of hurt, anger, and disappointment at this critical incident as a therapeutic error; but we consider the counselor's thoughts, feelings, and actions surrounding this incident as a necessary prelude to therapeutic change.

To further exemplify our point, the counselor in this instance had actually understood ahead of time that his client would experience disappointment and frustration in their relationship. The paradoxical therapeutic fact is that had the counselor maintained the posture of distance that this kind of generic diagnosis suggests, the relationship would never have matured to the point where the prediction could be emotionally confirmed and resolution of the conflict could occur. In other words, the counselor's ability to predict these consequences was essential to the relationship in the sense that it was his diagnostic skill that set the relationship on the proper course and activated the conflicted feelings. But the resolution of the client's conflicts could occur only in a relationship in which the emotional impact was associatively close to the feelings in the generic conflict.

THE IMPACT OF
CLIENT DYNAMICS AND CONFLICTS

Chapter 3

In this chapter, we will focus on the ways that clients experience, express, and resolve their conflicts in the developing and maturing counseling relationship. We are emphasizing the client's experience in the relationship to highlight the impact that the relationship effects in him. What does a client hope to derive from a relationship and yet what does he fear? How does he protect himself and yet reveal himself so that change can occur? And how is the client's ambivalence expressed and resolved in such a relationship?

Early in the chapter, we will describe the ways in which clients attempt to elicit responses from their counselors in order to effect certain goals. Since clients enter into counseling relationships in order to reduce discomfort and change themselves, they utilize eliciting behaviors to implement this goal. Yet, since change necessarily involves the experience of hurt and pain, the eliciting behaviors will also be utilized to avoid and defend against such anxiety-provoking experiences. We have noted in listening to therapeutic encounters that clients try to elicit behaviors from counselors which will help to correct their previous emotional experiences and will help them to change. But the dread of pain sometimes activates the clients to defend against experiencing anxiety by attempting to elicit responses which are intended to ward off the counselor's effectiveness and thus keep their conflicts intact.

The client's eliciting behaviors, therefore, reflect his ambivalence about whether he wants to change. The success of the counseling may depend on how intensely he communicates one side or the other of his ambivalence about changing. If the client's eliciting behaviors that were intended to ward off the counselor have been effective, then the client will feel unsatisfied and continue to attempt to manipulate his environment as a solution to his problems. Conversely, if the counselor has responded to the client's eliciting behaviors in a therapeutic way, then the client can begin to internalize his problem and begin the process of change.

Eliciting Behaviors: the principles

The eliciting behaviors are interpersonal methods that the client has learned as ways of coping with anxiety. The purpose for which the behaviors were learned and the reasons that the client still clings tenaciously to them is to ward off anxiety. Anxiety, therefore, is the emotional motivating force that runs through all of the eliciting behaviors. Although anxiety can be an experience related to many different conflicts, basically it arises out of the meaning that establishing and breaking human relationships has for a person. The motivation for the genesis and utility of the eliciting behaviors stems from a person's needs to manipulate and maintain interpersonal contacts and to avoid pain.

The eliciting behaviors were learned by the client as a result of previous interactions with persons who were significant to him. Since some of these interactions were hurtful, each person has developed ways of avoiding reexperiencing potentially hurtful relationships. But the paradox is that the behaviors that the person has learned in order to ward off close relationships carry with them the greater threat of abandonment and isolation. As a consequence of this second threat, behaviors have also usually been developed to maintain relationships. In this way, it can be seen that the eliciting behaviors are the behavioral manifestations of the client's interpersonal conflicts. On the one hand, he seeks closeness which could lead to possible pain; on the other hand, he seeks distance which could lead to possible isolation.

The eliciting behaviors have served to help the client avoid anxiety by coping satisfactorily with his interpersonal world. But their effectiveness has been weakened with resultant feelings of vulnerability and need for others. When the client is strong enough to counter the fear of being hurt, he may enter a counseling relationship. When the client enters the counseling relationship, he is openly confronted with the paradox of closeness or isolation because the counselor invites warmth and closeness which activate his fear about reexperiencing old hurts; and alternately he is equally restrained by the consequent fears of abandonment if he destroys the relationship or withdraws from it.

In this way, the counseling relationship is the fullest possible embodiment of the conflict and is the clearest interpersonal expression of the dual intent of the eliciting behaviors. Such a dynamic way of viewing the paradox of the eliciting behaviors makes explicable the apparently meaningless oscillation in the client's demands for closeness and distance which many counselors have experienced.

The dual intent of the eliciting behaviors reflects the ambivalence of the client about changing. On the one hand, the client may wish to avoid the pain of change and uses eliciting behaviors in an effort to repair the situation without exploring it since exploration involves pain. Since, however, the success of this kind of behavior also means lack of significant contact, warding-off behaviors arouse anxiety about isolation and this anxiety will activate eliciting behaviors which attempt to reestablish significant interpersonal contact.

The counseling process, then, can be viewed as one of oscillation between the client's attempts to elicit responses from the counselor which will reduce the counselor's effectiveness and attempts to mobilize the counselor. When the counselor is effective, the client will seek to avoid anxiety by trying to render the counselor ineffective; but when the relationship lags, the client will attempt to reactivate it. The client is constantly torn by anxiety arising out of what he fears will happen if his compressed feelings are expanded as opposed to counter fears about coping and being overwhelmed. Either of the dual intents may be uppermost in the client's eliciting behaviors at the time he enters the relationship. Whether the client attempts to activate or inhibit the relationship is a function of a number of things that we will enlarge on later.

A kind of eliciting behavior which demonstrates the attempt to immobilize the counselor is one which is a recurring theme with female clients who meet an aggressive male counselor. Often these clients will utilize a tremendous affective barrage involving highly dramatized speech, tears, and marked affective changes, all of which are intended to intensify the power of the communication that they are fragile and that any show of aggression on the counselor's part will be shattering to the client. Responding appropriately to this client's behavior is contingent on the counselor's awareness of the dynamic intent. Understanding the intent enables the counselor to formulate his response so that the client will expand the feeling underlying the defensive behavior.

The conflicts and dynamics of a client may be similar to those of other clients but the eliciting behaviors utilized may be quite different in any given counseling situation depending upon motivation at the time. One client, whose dynamics were similar to those of the case we have just described, but whose motivation was that of repairing and reestablishing a relationship, utilized eliciting behaviors which were aimed at revitalizing the relationship. This client went to considerable lengths to convince her wavering counselor that he was adequate and competent to work with her. The course of counseling in both the aforementioned cases was difficult. These difficulties will arise in the counseling relationship because of the subtle, complex interplay of both participants' dynamics.

For instance, clients who present themselves as being lonely, in need of friends, and without ready sources of emotional supplies are often quite appealing to counselors. The feelings and eliciting behaviors associated with these problems more readily touch on the nurturant needs of counselors than do clients whose initial eliciting behaviors are more hostile, negative, or disruptive. We wish to point out, however, that emotionally appealing clients will often disappoint and hurt the naïve counselor, even though the early portions of the relationship may be satisfying to both persons. Eventually the overtly "needy" client will react to his fears about the counselor's withdrawing and defending himself against the intensity of the early emotional relationship. Such an initially appealing client may even become quite distant, hostile, and destructive.

We have noted that clients with similar dynamics and with similar intentions to establish or disrupt a relationship may attempt to elicit quite different counselor responses. We were only able to explain these differences when we included the counselor's stimulus value in the equation. Since the eliciting behaviors are a many-sided internal-client concept of how to cope with his interpersonal world, it then becomes clear that the particular eliciting behaviors that are utilized by the client are a function of the dynamic interaction between client and counselor.

ELICITING BEHAVIORS: THE APPLICATIONS

In this section, we will integrate the various principles underlying the eliciting behaviors by applying them to specific cases. Through these cases, we will exemplify how the range and intensity of a client's eliciting behaviors reflect the client's resourcefulness and ability to cope with a counselor in maintaining distance and misdirecting the course of counseling. We have also observed in these cases that the richness of a client's repertoire of interpersonal coping behaviors is diagnostically productive of understanding the strength of the client and the level of his emotional development. In addition, we hope to explain how the choice of eliciting behaviors not only reflects a client's interpersonal skill but how it can give us some insight into the counselor's dynamics. Whether a client is effective in defending against a counselor and in misdirecting him is intricately interwoven with the counselor's own needs and dynamics as evidenced by his responses to the client.

Miss Paula—Eliciting Sympathy and Careful Treatment

Miss Paula's counselor approached their counseling relationship in the initial interview with great promise of potential understanding, and he directed the interview somewhat aggressively as though he were already insightful about her problems. Miss Paula immediately and repeatedly implied that she should be treated gently and with caution. Her major mode of defending against the counselor's approach to her was to suggest by content and her associated affect that she was "fragile" and would "break" easily. Miss Paula's choice of behavior in response to her counselor reflects her keen awareness of her counselor's initial behaviors toward her. Had a counselor approached this same client in a more passive way, we feel that she would have attempted to elicit more potent responses from him. Miss Paula's choice of behavior, then, directly reflects the interaction of both persons' dynamics.

These behaviors of Miss Paula were her attempt to control the counseling relationship and to maintain distance. But they represent only one aspect of the many eliciting behaviors that this client utilized as she sought to achieve and maintain distance with regard to various phases of her particular conflicts. When the counselor attempted to help Miss Paula to expand her feelings about her generic conflicts, Miss Paula warded off the counselor's exploration of her feelings by eliciting "collaboration" from the counselor with regard to her angry feelings about her mother.

Although we felt that the angry feelings were defensive and served to keep the relationship from developing along more productive lines, the counselor responded sympathetically to her demands for confirmation of her hostility towards her mother. We felt that the client's criticalness of her mother was associatively close to feeling neglected by the mother and that the counselor, in "collaborating" with the client, moved in the direction of helping her to rid herself of her mother oblivious to her underlying feelings of need for her mother.

Dynamically, this collaboration was therapeutically unproductive for other reasons since in this case destroying the mother served to activate conflicted feelings about her relationship with her father. The consequence of the counselor's acquiescence to what Miss Paula had elicited was that the relationship went into an unresolved cycle which accentuated depressed feelings and provoked additional fears and anxiety which could not be attached to anything meaningful. Put another way, the counselor, in acquiescing

to the client's eliciting behaviors, believed as she did that the solution to her conflicts lay in the expression of anger rather than in
understanding what she was angry about.

Miss Paula's expressed feelings of fragility, her accompanying
powerful affect, and her expressed need for collaboration all worked
together to convince the counselor that the appropriate therapeutic
endeavor was to respond sympathetically to what she was eliciting
rather than to explore the meaning of the needs. In this case, the
counselor saw the therapeutic venture as being one of responding
directly to the wants as expressed. Had the counselor been able
to attribute the defensive value to the eliciting behaviors and to
see them as compressed pieces of affect, he might have been able to
help the client to expand the associated feelings.

We have noted in listening to interviews that counselors are
often readily affected and immobilized by a client's demands to be
treated with undue caution. The immobilizing power of this particular eliciting behavior probably derives from the threat that the
counselor experiences about the projected consequences of his intervention into the client's life. If the client implies that he will fall
apart at the slightest provocation and the counselor literally believes the communication, his consequent feelings—inadequacy, omnipotence, anger—may interfere with his effectiveness.

Some clients are fragile; but we are suggesting here that the
message of fragility which is accompanied by many other indica-
tions of strength and adequacy should be considered for its probable
defensive value. Further, we are pointing out that the strength of
the affect in the communication presents a powerful enough threat
to a counselor so that he may lose sight of other client manifestations of strength. Provided that the counselor evaluates the behavior in terms of its intended impact, he may be enabled to cast
the behavior into a number of potentially therapeutic frameworks.

The counselor may, for example, begin to make his own associations to the kind of family constellation that was at the source
of these kinds of client needs. Further, he may wonder about the
kind of father such a client may have had. Did she perhaps enlist
her father as an ally in prior collaborations against the mother?
When the counselor begins to associate in such ways to the intended
meanings of the eliciting behaviors, he may recall that the demand

to be treated with gentleness followed closely on the heels of his own show of strength in the counseling relationship. This association may suggest to him that the client needs to explore possible conflicted feelings about strong males and consequent needs to distract them.

Mr. Phil—A "Fragile" Male

In the case just cited, a female client utilized fragility to immobilize a male counselor who behaved in a strong direct manner towards her. We have observed similar behavior on the part of male clients who have been confronted with the necessity of coping with female counselors. In the case of Mr. Phil, who presented himself as fragile to his female counselor, the potency of this particular eliciting behavior was again evident because the counselor was immediately and completely disarmed by the client's expressed fears of "shattering." The strength of the affect associated with Mr. Phil's message was sufficiently intense so that the counselor was unable to make a response which assumed enough client strength to deal with the underlying conflict. In effect, clients who use this type of eliciting behavior leave the counselor with no room to respond therapeutically if the counselor believes the message.

The intensity of Mr. Phil's initial way of presenting himself restrained the counselor from evaluating the fears as a guard against potential exploration of the client's conflicts. In addition, when the counselor has been immobilized, the client has gained control of the relationship and, as in this case, can then manipulate the counselor into helping him on his own terms. In this case, Mr. Phil saw only two alternative solutions to his problem and he was able to lead his counselor to believe that she must help him to choose between these alternatives rather than to explore the meaning of his conflicts with the consequent disorganizing effect that consideration of new or different alternatives might have.

This client's alternatives were, first, that he could stay at home and be infantile or alternatively that he must be completely separated from his family. Neither of these alternatives was palatable to the counselor since she recognized that both alternatives were manifestations of the same underlying conflict. Although the counselor was aware that the therapeutic process in this case should involve exploration and experience of the feelings associated with the underlying conflict, she was immobilized because of her fears about the client's fragility.

Counselor fears that a client will disintegrate or shatter if the client's conflicted feelings surface, as they inevitably will in an affective relationship, are not the only reactions which can immobilize a counselor. We have observed a number of variations on the theme of attempting to incapacitate a counselor through questioning his adequacy. Some clients directly challenge the adequacy of the counselor by questioning his qualifications to do the job. These direct challenges may be expressed by asking about the counselor's training and more or less subtly implying that the counselor will need to convince the client that he is adequate. This challenge and implication, if it is not recognized as such, may precipitate the counselor into an immediate effort to prove his adequacy rather than to recognize the dynamic intent of the challenge as revealing of the client's conflicts and ways of coping with people.

When a client attempts to communicate fragile behavior, he uses much associated affect to intensify the impact of the communication. In a similar way, when a client questions a counselor's adequacy, the client may also use a number of accompanying behaviors to insure eliciting the intended response. Clients may also challenge more subtly by suggesting that others have failed to be helpful, and, to emphasize the point, they may refer to prestige persons from their community who have attempted to help but failed.

Another very challenging eliciting behavior is that of the client who says, "I don't trust psychologists very much," or "I dislike prying people." This particular behavior may strike a counselor in a vulnerable spot because, in a sense, his whole ability to help people is based on their trust in him; and it is necessary for him to "pry" into the client's life in order to help him. We have noted that clients will supplement these kinds of behaviors by further implying that unless their demands are met, they will take flight from the relationship. The threat to take flight is, of course, distressing to the counselor since he has strong needs to be helpful and his professional adequacy is based on the premise that he can assist many of the people who need counseling.

Mr. Joe—Eliciting Interpretations and Rejection

Mr. Joe exemplifies the way a client can threaten a counselor's adequacy by subtle implications that, unless the counselor behaves in accord with the client's prescription, he will leave the relationship. Mr. Joe quite overtly challenged the counselor by suggesting that he was quite "transparent" and that most people were able to understand him quite readily. The counselor experienced these statements as a sufficiently strong challenge so that he responded in accord with the client's intent. Apparently the client's specific intention here was to get the counselor to be active and revealing about himself so that the client could then control the situation.

The client accomplished the distancing objective by making a number of premises about himself where a strong apparent meaning and probable conclusion were implied but not stated. Since the counselor had been challenged by Mr. Joe's opening remarks, the counselor was enticed into stating the most likely conclusion. The destructive intention of the client's behaviors becomes evident at these points since we have noted that these clients will then deny the relevance of the conclusion for their case. The ultimate effect here is that this counselor behavior confirms the client's hypothesis that people are inadequate to help him, and the client eventually leaves the relationship.

In listening to interviews where clients make such overt attempts to challenge the counselor in this particular way, we have been struck by the motives which seem to underlie such eliciting behavior. The eliciting behaviors, of course, are intended to precipitate reactions, and in such cases as Mr. Joe, the ultimate intent is to destroy the counseling relationship. Why and how does a person develop such interpersonal destructive behaviors? We believe, of course, that the behaviors have been developed as a consequence of earlier interpersonal relations with significant persons. What could the nature of these interactions have been? We suggest that such client behavior has been developed as an effective counter to hostile, aggressive, and rejecting behavior on the part of one or more past significant figures.

What the client has learned is that if he promises passivity in the face of aggression, he can often effectively provoke the aggression and that once the aggression is provoked he can then be destructive of the aggressor's adequacy by covert counteraggression or even by continued passivity. Thus what such persons as Mr. Joe do is to set up their interpersonal relationships with significant persons who are older, have authority, or are superior, so that these persons, as our client sees them, will lose their hurtful adequacy through exposure to the ridicule of being wrong. Once Mr. Joe had precipitated his counselor into exposing himself as we have described it, Mr. Joe then could leave the relationship since the counselor could now neither hurt nor help him.

We believe, then, that counselors can deal most effectively with such eliciting behaviors as Mr. Joe's by recognition of the purpose of the challenge. If the counselor can recognize the client's intent, then he can keep his needs to be adequate internal to himself and demonstrate his adequacy over time by helping the client to explore and expand the feelings he has about being such a transparent person.

Miss Anna—Eliciting Understanding and Help

We have noted the way that clients vacillate between their wishes to defend against change and their needs to change in a number of cases. Often, if the eliciting behaviors that are motivated by the client's wish to defend against change are successful, the client may blatantly reveal his deceptive purposes to the counselor in order to reactivate him. As an example, Miss Anna approached her male counselor in their initial contact by describing her conflicts with her parents and how her father in particular had refused to permit her to grow up. During the interview, Miss Anna sobbed, continually wrung her hands, and in a muted half-whispered tone described how her father was restraining her from being on her own.

Rather than to note the incongruity between the immaturity of the affect and the expressed wishes embedded in the client's statements, the counselor responded by allying himself with the client's expressed wish and openly sympathized with her in her fight against her parents. The counselor was apparently overwhelmed by the strength of her affect and, in overlooking the incongruity between the immaturity of the client's affect and her expressed wish to leave home, the counselor missed the real internal turmoil and the client's confusion about her emotional maturity.

The counselor's sympathetic behavior apparently stimulated fears in the client that the counselor would miss the internal experience of conflict entirely. Miss Anna changed her demeanor dramatically and she quite clearly indicated that she often cried to get what she wanted from her father. Had the counselor been free enough to do so, he might have associated the change in Miss Anna's verbal expressions and affect to the impact of his responses and then tracked the sequence of events in their encounter that had precipitated the change.

By tracking his own feelings that were stimulated by the interpersonal impact of the client's affect, he might have turned a therapeutic error into a powerfully corrective experience for the client. And, most assuredly, in the course of their relationship, as the counselor touches on conflicted areas, the client's ambivalence will be reactivated and she will attempt again and again to elicit responses which are geared to derail the counselor. At such points, the counselor's increased understanding of the meaning of the client's eliciting behaviors can enable him to respond in ways which will help the client to internalize the problem and ultimately to change.

INTERNALIZATION-EXTERNALIZATION:
A DIMENSION OF CLIENT EXPERIENCING

In the preceding section, we indicated that the eliciting behaviors are, in part, designed to enable the client to defend himself against more acute experiences of fear, anxiety, deprivation, and loss. One effective way in which clients manage this defense is by attributing the source of their difficulties, and even their own feelings, to the environment. The environment, for our purposes, consists primarily of significant persons in the client's past and present life who are seen by the client as the continuing source of his conflicted experiences.

While the client may be right that his problems have arisen as a consequence of his interactions with these persons and that his present, continuing interactions may be aggravating his feelings of conflict, we believe that the client often, if not always, holds an irrational premise about how to resolve his conflicts. This irrational premise consists, basically, of the notion that since these persons have been and are involved in the development of the client's problems, that the client can only change himself after these significant persons have been changed by his or someone else's efforts.

Realistically speaking, it is unlikely that parents, for instance, can be changed easily. Yet the battle which may have gone on for years is hard to give up, since the alternative is to change oneself which of necessity involves pain, anxiety, and much that is unknown. The greatest unknown is, of course, whether the change in one's self will be more satisfying in terms of the ensuing new kinds of responses from others. We believe, however, that for many clients the decision must be made, usually with the counselor's help, that this risk must be taken.

AVOIDING THE CONFLICT: ATTEMPTING EXPULSION

The kinds of conflicts that the client is experiencing, the learned modes of coping with his interpersonal world, the intensity of the client's needs to reorganize and change some of his feelings, and the ways that the client has learned to view himself interact in innumerable ways to affect the client's resiliency for changing. But basic to all of these ways of preventing change is the client's unwillingness to see the source of the problem as having its roots in his preconceptions of others and his behavior toward them.

To keep his problems externalized, a client may attempt to elicit sympathy from his counselor or to get him to identify with him instead of understanding and exploring the conflict. A client may attempt to attach his anxiety to some event or person in the environment and try to resolve the problem by putting distance between himself and the person. Clients may attempt to get the counselor to seduce them into counseling and thus confirm their hypotheses about the weaknesses and conflicts of significant persons.

These ways of warding off change, although defensive, suggest activity and some interpersonal maturity in the client. Clients may also utilize less mature defenses against experiencing their conflicts as internal. They may simply deny the problem, or they may project it onto the counselor or others. That is, they may contend that the parent is controlling them or that the institution has failed them.

Anxiety, which is fundamental to therapeutic change, can also serve as a defense against internalization. If, for example, anxiety is experienced in a free-floating state, the diffuse distress experienced by the client may ward off effective counseling. Even when anxiety is experienced as an internal, manageable state, the client may attach the anxiety to the wrong persons, experiences, or events and see the solution to his problem as being that of putting distance between himself and the perceived source of anxiety.

Conflicted feelings are often associated with the various developmental hurdles encountered in the complex process of growing up. Since at these significant points both the culture and the family may dictate what the appropriate solutions are to be, clients are likely to externalize their problems and feelings insofar as any given developmental task has been unsuccessfully mastered. This tendency to externalize can often be clearly seen in adolescents and young adults as they ambivalently struggle with the need to maintain the comforting security of home and family and the conflicting need to have an independent life. The college or high school client often sees and defines this problem in a way which, for many, makes the resolution of the problem apparently impossible.

On the one hand, such a client may experience much anxiety about his own control over himself and the problems he may incur if he gives free rein to his impulses. He might still wish much help from parents and from the institution in regard to controlling and safeguarding him. On the other hand, the client may also experience parental and institutional curbs, real or imagined, as unduly restricting and may even perceive the solution to the problem as ridding himself of these restraints entirely.

Such a client will often attempt to persuade his counselor, by a burst of angry affect, that the way to resolve his conflict and its associated anxiety is by "tearing out" his parents' continuing influence on him. Counselors may respond to such eliciting behavior in a number of ways. However, the client by the very intensity of his affect may lead the counselor to believe that the contradictory solutions, as the client perceives them, are the only alternatives available.

One counselor may choose to try to reinforce the "control" alternative, perhaps as the client's parents have done. A counselor may attempt this projected resolution by pointing out to the client, more or less subtly, that the client should behave himself. Such a counseling effort may well be met with hostility, passive resistance, or acquiescence; but the counselor may well feel that he has not been very effective no matter what response the client makes. Another counselor may try to help the client to realize the solution to his problem by supporting and encouraging the client's anger. This counselor may then be astonished to find that his efforts seem to be aggravating the conflict in ways he doesn't understand.

The difficulty, in one way, with both of these approaches to the problem is that the client does not really wish to choose either alternative. Also, neither approach gives the client credit for internal strengths and capacities he may well have for the development and ultimate adoption of new and better alternatives for solving his conflict. Finally, these counselor approaches serve to keep the client's conflicts externalized along with the ensuing continued feelings of anger, frustrating hurt, and impotence.

Counselor responses which assume that the client can expand the feelings associated with his conflicts not only reflect his faith in the client's capacities, but are also more effective in enabling the client to internalize his problems. The expansion of feelings, which is the basic means for internalizing, may, of course, lead to a fulmination of feelings of conflict. This is the counseling objective, however, since the acute experience of conflict as internal to one's self is the necessary emotional prelude to the development of new alternatives and new internally felt means of control. Parents and other perceived sources of conflict can then be incorporated and integrated in new ways and even experienced as meaningful and helpful in the continuous unfolding of life.

Miss Portia—Preventing Internalization

The case of Miss Portia will assist us to understand better how a counselor can collaborate with a client to continue externalization of a problem. In the first interview, the client elicited a sympathetic response from the counselor. He apparently believed too easily that her anger toward her father, in particular, was totally justified and that the solution to her problem was to expel and get rid of the father. The counselor implemented his conclusion by encouraging her anger and commenting several times to the effect that her parents were mean to her.

A literal interpretation of and collaboration with a client's anger in early interviews may be therapeutically nonproductive since such behavior obscures the meanings and antecedents of the anger. Our observation is that, in general, anger is a consequent or reactive feeling rather than an original feeling experience.

Perhaps as a consequence of the counselor's collaboration with the client's angry feelings in the first interview, Miss Portia began in her next few interviews to express guilt feelings in relationship to her father. She may even have felt guilty about being able to deceive the counselor. The counselor, rather than helping the client to explore and expand why she might be feeling guilty, persisted in believing that she must be rid of her father for he was now seen as the source of the guilty feelings. By persisting in blaming the father, the counselor may actually have augmented the client's conflict.

Miss Portia did begin, as we have suggested earlier, to attempt to reorient the counselor by alluding to deprived, hurt feelings which she experienced in relationship to her father. She suggested that perhaps some of this hurt might derive from her father's inability to care about her. Did she then mean that the counselor, too, was not caring appropriately about her?

Since in this case, the counselor was unable to reinterpret his understanding of the client's communications, the client terminated the relationship by simply not returning for subsequent interviews. As a consequence of the lack of expansion of this client's feelings and conflicts, we are unsure of many of the meanings of this counselor and client interaction. However, we do suspect that this client may have rejected the counselor because she concluded that he, like her father, had not taken the time to understand or care sufficiently about her feelings and conflicts.

Avoiding the Conflict: attempting
compression

Earlier, we spoke of the way that a client may have compressed affect and content of experiences into compacted statements that represent the ways he feels about himself. By encapsulating the feelings and perhaps by overlaying them with many distortions, the client wards off experiencing the impact of the generic conflict. To facilitate internalization and resolution of client conflicts, the counselor needs to be alert to and eventually to learn to read the compacted content of the interviews, sentences, and even the words that the client uses to symbolize his life experiences.

Clients' abilities to symbolize their experience in this kind of cognitive way and the relative impermeability of their defenses vary. But unless the encysting threads of the compacted feelings are unwoven, thus facilitating the expansion of experiences, the counseling relationship will terminate with both client and counselor feeling dissatisfied as a result of having undergone a significant interpersonal failure.

Alternately stated, the words and phrases that the client has come to use to symbolize himself represent a structure that he has spun around himself to protect himself from affective reactivity to previous significant experiences. The client has approached the counseling relationship because the symbolic representation of his life experiences has come to be an ineffectual resolution of con-flicted behaviors and some of the encysted feelings are stirring.

A given word, used repetitively and within similar contextual clues, often represents such a "compacted experience." The signifi-cance of the meaning of the word, can, however, only become an effective instrument in helping the client to change if the counselor is willing to hold in abeyance the culturally defined meaning of the word and assume that the client may be using the word in a highly idiosyncratic way and that the word may be the client's disguise for traumatic personal experiences. We have observed that when clients refer to themselves as "degraded," as having been "angelic children," or when they refer to feelings they have of "suffocation" or "bursting," that these words, when expanded, open up vistas of previous significant experiences. Often, these experiences center around the client's behavior toward significant persons or the behavior of those persons toward them which was disruptive enough of their normal development that the clients had to protect the associated reactive feelings from themselves by hiding behind a highly intellectualized label.

Just as the client used the symbol to defend against his feelings, so, too, the counselor may choose to protect himself. We have noted that some counselors may avoid the experience of exploring the meaning underlying the experience expressed by a word because they can not tolerate the exploration themselves. At other times the counselor's need to nurture the client may override his therapeutic skill, and he may want to reassure the client that he does not feel that he is "degraded." Such reassurance may help the client to experience this relationship as a warm one and the counselor as a person who wants to help because the feelings are motivated by nurturance. But it is difficult to determine how much of a source of influence such counselor behavior may have on the client in terms of eventual change.

But, the counselor should realize that such reassurance arises out of his own system of needs to nurture rather than out of what the experience of degradation means to the client. By reassuring the client, the counselor has attributed his own meaning, that is, the culturally determined meaning of the word without understanding the client's meaning. As a consequence, the counselor may have inadvertently communicated a double message to the client. On the one hand, he communicates a wish to help; but he also communicates a wish to quiet troubled waters without stirring them up enough to see what is at the source of the disquiet. Such reassurance, in other words, simultaneously communicates a wish to approach and a wish to avoid the client. As we have often noted in our listening, the source of the client's ambivalence about his inter-personal relationships and his conflicts have often arisen precisely out of this type of "push-pull" relationship with other significant persons in his past.

There are a number of other pitfalls to assuming the meaning of the words the client is using without attending to the word by insisting that the client explicate it. When the counselor assumes the meaning, he does so from his own connotative system which has a wider meaning than the dictionary supplies. For exam-ple, a counselor may supply his own meanings to the words that the client is using and may become anxious as a result of what he interprets the words to mean. A client in presenting himself may report that he is very "peculiar" and "far out." The coun-selor's assumption that the client's behaviors are socially deviant ones based on the words that the client uses to describe himself is an unfounded one unless the counselor assesses the meanings these words have for the client.

The point is that the counselor needs to find out what "acting peculiarly" means to the client, rather than to assume its meaning. The anxiety in this case has gotten transferred to the counselor when he supplied his own meanings, and in supplying his own meanings the counselor has inappropriately taken on the client's anxiety. The counselor's anxiety may be a function of his wondering whether the client's "peculiar" behaviors suggest possible organic problems or more severely pathological ones than he had supposed; and he may even begin to think of referring the client to a qualified physician.

An alternative approach to assuming the meaning for the client is to view the counseling function as one of recovering the concrete behaviors that were somehow merged together to form the highly symbolic and compacted words that the client uses to represent his experience. The counselor using this approach may discover that the client's meaning really refers to some behavior that is quite dif-ferent from what he had supposed. The richness of the therapeutic venture often resides in expanding the client's motivations for need-ing to revert to words with such potentially dramatic connotations instead of describing his problems in more honest but perhaps less colorful terms.

THE COUNSELOR:
A Human Being Who Helps

Chapter 4

We believe counselors help their clients by being human. How could this be? What do we mean by such a statement? Don't counselors help people because they are trained? Doesn't the fact that they are trained mean that counselors understand themselves completely and hence are free of the conflicts, defenses, and needs that their clients find so burdensome, troubling, and disorganizing?

We agree that counselors need training. But, in many ways, we think of good training as being of the sort which leads counselors to be most human. The counselor, as in any other occupation, has primarily himself to bring to the helping relationship. He may learn of technical aids such as tests; he may learn interviewing techniques; he may read widely and copiously about people; he may search desperately for a philosophy or an orientation; he may even attempt to copy the behaviors of those who are regarded as experts. Yet, ultimately, what he brings to his encounters with his clients is himself.

In our view, the counselor presents himself as a person who has lived, experienced conflict, more or less resolved some of his problems, and who experiences needs to help others with their problems. What does the counselor's training, then, do for him? As we have indicated, it may make him more knowledgeable about people in an abstract sense, about technical aids, and about ways of approaching people that may be helpful. Ultimately, however, we believe that it is the counselor's own life experience which is both the greatest asset and the greatest obstacle to his efforts to induce change in his clients.

His training should, we think, help him to know that his own life and his own person with his personal strengths, knowledge, weaknesses, conflicts, and needs can be potentially useful or harmful to his clients. His training, then, should set him on the road to discriminating how it is that the various aspects of his own person, as expressed in his relationships with his clients, can either facilitate or stalemate his clients' struggles to change. The counselor's personal self and how this self can and does express itself in counseling relationships is the subject matter of this chapter.

THE PARADOX OF CONTROL

Some persons wander through life attempting to control the behaviors of everyone they meet, and their lives reflect a succession of panic-ridden attempts to keep others in line. Their frantic efforts to manipulate the behavior of others stems from the fact that they experience the source of control for their own impulses as residing in others and they attempt to achieve resolution of their own conflicted feelings by manipulating others. Such persons maintain the myth that if they can only get others to behave in prescribed ways toward them then everything will be all right again. Their lives reflect their view of the environment and everyone in it as a puppet stage and, so long as they can manage all of the strings of the various puppets in their environment, they are comfortable enough and maintain good control over their impulses.

The control, in these cases, is achieved at great expense to the puppeteer's interpersonal relationships because the persons in his environment experience the intensity of his attempts to manipulate them in order to protect himself. Such relationships, although they achieve the purpose of maintaining controls, also achieve the concomitant goal of removing the manipulating person from any kind of warm contact with others in his environment.

When new persons enter such a person's environment, it becomes necessary for him to attempt immediately to attach the puppet strings to the intruders and to somehow incorporate them into the scheme of things. If these new persons react against being strung in with the group, then the person may begin to experience some anxiety, and as more and more of the puppets begin to behave in uncontrollable ways, the person's own controls, since they are externalized and experienced through the puppets, weaken and he becomes flooded with fears that his own behavior will become unmanageable.

At points like this in the person's life, he may request help from a counselor. When he first enters the relationship, the person's intention may be to find out how to repair the broken puppet strings or to find better ways of stringing the new puppets in with the group so that the stage is again set. The counselor may actually feel that the person's emotional state is in sufficient jeopardy to warrant his helping him to find new ways of manipulating his environment to again achieve a state of comfort. On the other hand, the counselor may feel that the vulnerability of the person is such that if he can use it sensitively, he may be able to help the person to develop interpersonal relationships that are more mature.

Although this may be the counselor's conscious choice, actually effecting such a change in the person is far from an easy task since the person has grown up with the childlike fiction that the successful maintenance of his emotional life is a function of controlling others. He will attempt almost immediately to try to control the counselor. The strength of his need to externalize his controls will determine the strength of the kinds of behaviors that he tries to elicit from the counselor. The unknown dimensions of the counseling relationship will most assuredly activate the client's need to structure the relationship. His need will be expressed in frantic attempts to illuminate the darkened corners of the relationship so that he can capture or recapture control of the situation.

The client's needs to control the counselor's behavior will be stronger than his needs to control many other persons because the stature of the counselor represents a more significant threat to loss of control. If the client is unable to control the counseling situation, a most significant part of his environment will go unstructured and therefore uncontrolled; and the prospects of his filling that void with uncontrolled impulses must certainly lead to a panic-stricken state in the client. Whether or not the counselor helps the client to repair the strings of his puppets or whether he helps the client to change and reexperience the puppets as real persons who have feelings and wishes that are independent of the client's feelings depends, among other things, on the counselor's assessment of the client's strength to tolerate the unknown as he learns that the ultimate source of control really does reside in himself.

If the counselor, too, experiences the world as a puppet stage and has control problems of his own, the chances are strong that when the client attempts to elicit behaviors from him to keep the client's own world intact the counselor will acquiesce and behave in accord with the client's wishes. When both the counselor and the client get enmeshed in the same control struggle, then the ensuing relationship would seem doomed to failure.

How expansive this relationship can become and how corrective the emotional experience can be for the client is a function, therefore, of how strongly the counselor needs to control the client in his explorations of his problems. A counseling relationship is a controlled environment, it is true, but it is not necessarily a controlling environment. The counselor controls the environment in the sense that he establishes the conditions of strength and consistency which the client has not experienced in the past in order to permit the client the necessary freedom to explore his conflicted feelings. Paradoxically, it is only because the environment that the counselor creates in their relationship is a strong, safe one, and in those respects a controlled one, that the client experiences the freedom to reshape his emotional life.

It is not a question, therefore, of whether the counseling relationship is a controlled one; it is rather a question of the appropriateness of the controls that are imbedded in the relationship. When the counselor's controls are a function of his inability to tolerate the exploration which the client can tolerate and which is necessary to help the client to change, then the counselor's motivations for attempting to control are suspect.

The key to unraveling the paradox of control resides, therefore, in understanding the source, nature, and motivations of the controls that are imbedded in a counseling relationship. Individual manifestations of the "control" problem may be quite varied; yet the needs to control may be motivated by quite similar dynamics. A client may enter a counseling relationship because he experiences some anxiety about the effectiveness of his controls. He may express his fears in a number of ways, but such a client often experiences some vague concern about behaving in socially undesirable kinds of ways unless someone controls him. Initially, such a client may perceive the counseling process as being one in which the counselor somehow directly and magically is able to control him. In fact, the client's entrée into the relationship may be an open request for such control.

The lives of these clients reflect a continuous search for someone to control them. Often the client's home situation is one in which the controls were constantly imposed by one or the other of his parents, and he never learned what his feelings were or what the constructive or destructive impact of his impulses might be. His parents' fears about their own impulses may have led them to impose controls on their child as a way of warding off their being confronted by the child's impulse life. Consequently, if the parent expressed so much concern about the child's impulses, the child may grow up with mixed feelings about how powerful and bad these feelings must be. Or, the converse could have obtained, and the child may have been arrested developmentally because one or the other of his parents may have been impulsive, thus leaving the task of controlling the parent as well as himself to the child.

In either case, the client may enter a counseling relationship with many fears that if he permits himself to feel certain ways he will most certainly overwhelm the counselor and himself in the process. Because of the fears about how potent his impulses are, he may be able to express his feelings only if he can continue to feel that the counselor is strong enough to control his actions.

If the counselor falls into the trap of believing that he is the receptacle of the client's controls, then the client must face the rather gloomy prospect of continually needing to seek out the counselor or an unending line of other parent surrogates as new variants of old impulses seek expression. In order to be helpful to the client the counselor must believe that he is sufficiently in control of himself so that he will not be overpowered by the client's feelings. If the counselor can believe this and behave accordingly, he will have reversed the client's previous significant emotional experiences.

By behaving in a strong, consistent way with the client, and by being sensitive to what the client is experiencing, the counselor will have created a relationship wherein the client can test out some of the feelings that he was never permitted to experience, much less express, in his earlier developmental years. Drawing on the strength of the relationship, the counselor can then assist the client to relearn something more of the meaning of his feelings, and the client can learn how to bring his impulses under his own control.

Another person may have impulse problems that seem quite different from those of the client discussed above. Whereas the latter was over-controlled, the former may actually be acting on his impulses and may be meeting repeated admonitions from various agents of societal norms. When he enters the counseling relationship, he may almost immediately threaten the counselor with "acting out" his behaviors if the counselor attempts to control him.

This client is not so different from the other as he might seem. Dynamically, the first client may conceal a variety of wishes and feelings by experiencing them as fears of potential power and destructiveness; but the second client conceals his feelings equally well from himself by acting on impulse and thus getting rid of the threat before he can "know" about it. He, too, believes, that the source of his controls is in others. He copes with his controls reactively, it is true, but he nonetheless believes that his parents and other authority figures supply the restraints. Although the first kind of client approaches the relationship by attempting to mobilize the counselor, the second client tries to control the situation by immobilizing the counselor. Both clients attempt to solve their discomfort by attempts at controlling and manipulating others. Both clients still see their problems as existing externally and try to solve their problems by manipulating the environment.

A client who threatens to behave in socially unacceptable ways is particularly troublesome to some counselors. The trouble stems from the counselor's believing that the client's problem requires that he assume the role of the controlling agent as others have attempted to do. If the counselor sees the solution to the problem as that of his directly attempting to control the client, he will, for a number of reasons, probably be unable to deal with the conflicted feelings subsumed under the client's threatening behaviors. For one thing, the counselor must invariably feel inadequate from the outset because, even if he is inclined to want to control, he does not have the control weapons to wield that some social agencies have, nor does he have any reason to believe that his admonitions will be heeded any more than have the scoldings and warnings of the client's parents, institutions, and other social agents. The counselor's training prepares him to explore the client's conflicted feelings, and his feelings of adequacy in working with the client are a function of his utilizing these professional skills.

We think that "acting out" behavior often represents a type of eliciting behavior which sets out to achieve, and is usually successful, one specific goal—that of threatening the counselor sufficiently to immobilize him as an effective therapeutic agent by redirecting his efforts into behaving precisely the way that everyone else does. Under the stress of such a threat, the counselor's response patterns may become quite limited and, depending upon his own dynamics, they may take one of several alternatives.

An aggressive counselor who experiences control problems of his own may respond to his own anxiety by reprimanding the client. The chances are that this kind of behavior on the part of the counselor will do no more than increase the client's eagerness to act out since the counselor is behaving in ways identical with other social agents. On the other hand, the counselor may respond to the threat by possibly disregarding the client's behavior and thereby hoping to assume no guilt for whatever behavior the client engages in. Either form of counselor behavior represents a defense against the counselor's own feelings, whatever they may be—guilt, fear, pleasure—and merely reflects a different control alternative.

The fact is that the counselor's own feelings may be disturbing enough to him so that he loses his grasp of the dynamics underlying the expressed attitude, and he attempts to absolve himself or abdicate his responsibility for helping the client with the conflict underlying the behavior. In either case, the counselor's behavior is reminiscent of the ways that the client's parents have probably behaved with him; and the lesson he has had reinforced is that this counselor, like his parents and other significant persons, is also fearful of his feelings. To whom can such a client now turn to explore and discover those essential parts of his emotional life that are cut off from him?

The solution to the control of "acting out" behaviors lies most often in the client's own exploration and understanding of his own motives, rather than in the counselor's ineffectual attempts at controlling such behavior. Inadequate controls are certainly a problem for the client, but ultimately the sources of control reside in the client and their availability is a function of whether the conflicted feelings which underlie the threat are explored.

The counselor's best defense against the client's threat to "act out" is ordinarily to consider the threat as an eliciting behavior whose aim is to ensure that his response will be an impotent attempt at control. If the counselor reflects on the power of the threat and its effectiveness in eliciting the intended response, he will have some insight into how powerful must be the deeper conflict that the client is warding off. In addition, as long as the meaning of the client's impulses is not available to him, he is most vulnerable to acting on impulse. By understanding the intensity of the client's inner struggle and the vulnerability of his present state, the counselor may be able to tolerate his own anxiety. And, to his astonishment, when he frees himself of fears that the client will act out, the counselor may find that the client's acting out behaviors diminish appreciably.

Only after the counselor decides to give up trying to control the client and lends his strength to the relationship can the client experience the relationship as a safe enough place to reveal his secrets. But, as we said much earlier, an emotional commitment to help a person to change is not a once-and-for-all event because the counselor is continually confronted with a range of client behaviors that may reactivate his need to control his own anxiety at the expense of helping the client.

An equation can probably be devised between the extent of the counselor's need to control a client and his own unresolved conflicts that lie in the same areas as the client's. And, the eventual lack of productivity of a relationship can probably be predicted from the extensiveness and variety of the restrictions that the counselor needs to place on a client in the explorations of his problems. The extensiveness of the controls that the counselor needs to exert not only reflects the tone of the relationship, but where a considerable number of controls are employed, it becomes increasingly apparent that the counselor's purpose is to make the relationship safe for himself and not the client.

Every relationship has built in safety valves because the participants are almost sure to experience some ambivalence toward each other as new areas are explored, as new threats are experienced, and as old struggles are recharged. But when the scales are tipped so that the safety essential for the client to grow is subtly converted into safety to permit the counselor to counsel, the relationship will inevitably be threatened. The question, then, of effective counseling is partly a matter of how easily frightened a counselor is of a client's affect and how easily his own conflicts are activated and immobilize him.

THE SEXUAL THREAT: ELICITING THE EROTIC RESPONSE

Many late adolescents and young adults enter counseling because they experience conflicts about their sexual feelings and behavior. We have observed that counselors, on the other hand, sometimes experience their greatest personal threat when they are confronted with the prospect of helping a client explore his conflicts in the areas of sexual fantasies, feelings, and behaviors. It is in this area more than in any other that a counselor may struggle with his own ambivalence about being helpful.

The counselor's ambivalence may be activated by a number of events in the relationship. If a counselor is working with a client of the opposite sex, his impressions of the client may be such that he finds the client so physically attractive that he may be inhibited by the power of his own fantasies. Or, the source of the client's conflicts may stimulate the counselor's own fantasies and awaken new or reawaken old conflicts. We have also observed that the client's expressed urgency about sexual feelings may distract the counselor from the exploration of the underlying dynamics, and he may attempt to short circuit the counseling process in an effort to control the client's current behaviors.

In all of these cases, the direction that the therapeutic venture will take is questionable because the counselor probably has responded by actively controlling the client's behavior. The counselor's response may have been governed by his own erotic impulses. The counselor needs to search out the dynamic meaning of his erotic feelings and fantasies and to associate them to what has occurred in his relationship with this client. The relationship will probably not be therapeutic for the client unless the counselor does so; and as the counseling sessions continue, the counselor may attempt increasingly to control what the client experiences and explores as a safeguard against his own impulsivity. Such counselor control may deprive the client of the opportunity to explore, know, and understand the meanings and implications of his own feelings and behaviors.

As in all cases, we can infer the intensity of the counselor's own inner experiences from the lengths that he may need to go to protect himself. Under stress, the counselor may retreat to the task of spending much of his time with the client in the construction of a series of barriers against closeness. We are not suggesting that a counselor does not need to develop defenses against the threat of a client's sexual needs; but we are suggesting that if the counselor's defenses are distancing ones, the relationship is likely to deteriorate.

We have observed a number of defenses that are often used by counselors as a means of keeping their impulses in check. To defend against the intensity of his own feelings, the counselor may interpret the client's feelings or behaviors before the affect is clearly enough experienced by the client for an interpretation to have any kind of emotional impact. In fact, such a premature response will have an emotional impact of the wrong kind on the client, for it may do no more than to reinforce the client's feelings about the power of the stimulus value of his sexuality. And the client will have relearned in this relationship that his fears about his sexual feelings are true: his feelings are powerful enough to overwhelm someone who the client must certainly feel ought to be less vulnerable to the eliciting effect of his behaviors and more incisive about the dynamic meaning of the behavior.

A counselor may also attempt to ward off being confronted with the client's mature sexuality by inducing regression in the client. Only if the client is willing to relate to him as a little girl or boy is the counselor willing to deal with his sexual concerns. Such a counselor defense places severe stress on the relationship and places inappropriate demands on the client because it drains the client's resources in order to make the relationship safe for the counselor. Since we believe that client regression can be therapeutically necessary for change to occur or destructive if regression is motivated by the wrong reasons, we have devoted another section to discussing its merits and problems.

Effecting client regression or making premature interpretations are just two ways that a counselor may defend against experiencing the sexual threat. If a client is sexually aggressive, the counselor may also attempt to distance the relationship by depersonalizing the conflict. He may achieve this goal by shifting his frame of reference and alluding to the client and to the client's conflicts in the third person as though the conflicts really existed independent of the two of them. Rather than asking his client, "What are your fears about sex?" the counselor wonders with the client what the client's fears are. Instead of being confronted by this client and his feelings, the counselor is then able to counsel the mythical character that he has created. If the client plays the game, then both have profited and lost. The counselor is insulated against being touched by his client, and his client, in turn, has found a wonderful depersonalized scapegoat on which to project his conflicts. Neither participant risks anything, but neither does change occur.

Desexualizing a client is another form of avoiding the risk of human encounter. Attempts of male counselors to "masculinize" their female clients represent the most blatant example of this counselor defense; attempts to identify or collaborate with the client's problems are perhaps more subtle manifestations. The phenomenon of desexualizing a client most often occurs at those points in the counseling relationship when sexual material and sexual conflicts are in the foreground of the client's explorations. The threat of the sexual encounter on a mature genital level can often be sufficiently disturbing to the counselor so that he attempts to reduce the threat at any expense to himself or his client.

The male counselor's intention here is not the same as it is when he attempts to induce regression or depersonalize. His intention is to change her sex and thus to alleviate the heterosexual threat. Subtle, but unavoidably clear, the counselor's language betrays his intention here for it reflects the masculine attributes with which he wishes to cloak his client. When his female client has met academic success, he may refer to her success as her "batting a thousand," or when she copes aggressively with her peers, he may refer to her behavior as "hitting the line."

The male counselor who uses such a defense against his client's femininity achieves his own tension reduction at great expense to the client because the sexual conflict that brought her into the counseling relationship in the first place reflects poor sexual identification, and such counselor language and behavior certainly must cause the client to wonder about her identity. We noted an interesting sequence of events in the relationship of a counselor who attempted to masculinize his female client. It increased our belief that not only does this type of counselor defense exist, but that it may also effect possibly dire consequences in the client's emotional life.

In this particular case, the counselor was sufficiently threatened by the client's mature sexual overtures toward him that his language revealed his anxiety and wish to desexualize her. The client must have experienced a powerful threat to her identity, for she almost immediately attempted to recapture her femininity again. The client began to talk, with no manifest verbal linkage, of a boy that she had recently met and whom she planned to marry. She then proceeded to cry and to behave in very helpless, feminine ways in the relationship.

This behavior on her part we felt was interesting from several points of view. For one thing, the client's unconscious must have told her that her seductive behavior was beginning to threaten the counselor, so she dredged up a male toward whom she could legitimately have sexual feelings, thus relieving the counselor of his threat. Having made the relationship safe, her next statements were attempts to elicit nurturance from the counselor. And, since she had now made herself safe by being "spoken for," she could elicit nurturance toward herself as a female and thus restore her identity.

Our insight into the meaning of these client behaviors was derived from our examining the sequence of events in the relationship. First, the client attempted to satisfy her needs for being nurtured by behaving seductively toward the counselor. The counselor's language reflected his attempt to distance and drastically restructure their relationship. The threat of distancing the relationship before she had had her needs satisfied must have terrified the client for her response was to introduce another male and thus make the relationship safe enough so that she could have several needs satisfied: she could be treated as a female and experience a warm relationship.

One of the counselor's best defenses against the client's sexual demands or his own fantasied projections of these demands is to consider the probable development of a person who needs to use sexuality so blatantly in a relationship. In the case of a female client with a male counselor, the client must have learned very early that if she behaves in seductive ways she is more apt to elicit rewarding responses from males than if she appeals directly without implying her availability in the bargain. The client's experiences must have been that in order to get any of her needs satisfied, she needed to disguise the genuine needs and hope to satisfy them indirectly and only contingently on an adequate display of sexual overtones. Basic to her earlier needs are the needs for affection and approval from her earlier significant relationships which have probably gone unsatisfied, and many of the needs the client now experiences are derivatives of those earlier unsatisfied needs.

When a female client enters a counseling relationship, she may have many layers of needs that she wishes to express—she has needs to achieve academically, needs to develop a career, needs to be recognized by peers, needs to be sought after for marriage. But the client enters the counseling relationship still clinging to the belief that the only way she can satisfy these needs is to subvert them under strong sexual overtones. The earlier lesson that this client has probably also learned is that she can avoid facing some difficult tasks and can manipulate men to get what she wants by using her sexuality. The general developmental lesson she has learned is that her seductiveness is the avenue to her need satisfaction.

It is inevitable that such a client will almost immediately begin to cope with the counselor as she has with other males by using herself sexually in the relationship to elicit help or to distract the counselor from helping. The client's seductiveness can carry alternative consequences for the course of counseling if it is the only avenue available to the person for fulfilling her needs. The unfortunate fact regarding the client's resourcefulness is that when such a person is unsuccessful in satisfying her needs by her more usual covert seductive means, she will just become more blatant and strident in her attempts at seduction instead of attempting to elicit help by invoking alternative coping behaviors. On the other hand, the client's limited repertoire can have catalytic effects on the client's process of changing her behavior, and her blatancy may bring her conflicts into bold relief.

REGRESSION: COUNSELOR OR CLIENT NEED?

Understanding and changing one's self often, if not always, involves reexperiencing earlier feelings and conflicts with the sharpness, probable pain, and clarity of those earlier experiences. Clients, since they have powerful coping capacities, have usually defended themselves with some success against experiencing past feelings in their present lives. The partial breakdown or malfunctioning of these defense mechanisms with the consequent "leaking" of earlier affective experiences is often what brings the client into a counseling relationship.

At the point the client enters counseling he is necessarily ambivalent about whether he will or wants to continue the regression which has begun into his own past. He may deeply fear that he will be overwhelmed by the further reexperiencing of the earlier feelings and that he will not recover. The fears and anxiety associated with the actual or perceived threat of regression may lead the client to make powerful demands on the counselor to help with the restoration of his defenses.

Counselors may, of course, accede to these demands because it appears that the client might not, in fact, be able psychologically to survive his regression. Also, however, counselors may be deceived by powerfully expressed client fears about anticipated regression in particular. Such clients may well be able to lead counselors to overlook obvious client resources for handling and profiting from the reexperiencing of powerful prior affective experiences. Interestingly, clients who have adequate resources to bear such reexperiencing and to reap the benefits of change which may ensue will usually attempt to reorient the counselor whom they may themselves have successfully misled.

We believe, then, that regression may very often be the antecedent to change. Further, we believe that most persons have the capacity to tolerate and utilize regression and that they will often themselves be aware of this route to change. Client defense against regression may always be present, however, and should be understood by the counselor as such.

Besides being a means to change, client regression usually has other meanings to both client and counselor. Regression, once accomplished by the client, may be found by both participants to be a comfortable and even rewarding state. The client, for instance, may enjoy being dependent and childlike and will express with powerful affect his indefinite continuing need for nurturance. It is at such a point that a counselor can again experience much conflict. Should he believe that his client's dependent needs are this great? Will the client really collapse if he withdraws as the client may be suggesting he will?

We observe that often counselor belief that the implication of either question is true may be an error, or perhaps, a reflection of the counselor's own needs. If the counselor literally believes the client's dependent needs are as real as the client implies, then the counselor may feel omnipotent or, possibly, angry and rejecting since he must necessarily feel that he cannot meet such powerful needs for succorance. In either case, the counselor errs, in part, by assuming present and continuing reality in regard to the client's feelings. Further, the counselor is assuming that he has responsibility for the generic conflict and that he must fulfill the role of the client's parent.

The client, of course, has the right to voice any demands he feels. The counselor should, of necessity, retain his own autonomy and consequent right to choose how he will respond. As long as he is in a position to choose his own alternatives rather than the client's, the counselor maintains his own adequacy which will enable him to respond appropriately so that the client can change and mature. Strangely enough, if the counselor believes the client's alternatives, he has become the client's inadequate parent who failed originally.

Counselor needs, dynamics, and conflicts may affect client regression in other ways. Counselors, we believe, have a need to nurture. Yet such counselor needs may also involve beliefs about what kinds of persons it may be safe to nurture. The male counselor with a female client may feel, for instance, that he can safely nurture females who are childlike but may be much threatened if his client is perceived as a sexually mature woman. Such a conflict may lead the counselor to force undue or unneeded regression in the client to insure the counselor's safety. Or the counselor may actively resist a client's efforts to grow up since such maturity may rouse the sexual threat.

Counselor needs to nurture may function in another way to interfere with client growth and change. The nurturant need in the counselor may demand immediate satisfaction. Such needs for immediate reward may lead to unneeded regression or to counselor efforts to maintain regressed states. Dependent clients are rewarding in the sense that they express most clearly their need for the counselor. It is as though the counselor will lose his source of gratification if his client matures and the relationship is eventually terminated.

Actually, such a counseling relationship, if maintained long enough, leads to a psychological reversal of roles where the client may actually be doing the nurturing. In such a case, the client may adopt behavior and ways of speaking which are revealing of the distressing turnabout. Miss Mary, for example, spoke of feeling "hollow" and "drained" without being able to attach the feelings to any present or past circumstances in her life. For her to have recognized consciously the stimulus for her feelings would apparently have been too threatening.

Miss Mary tried to resolve her dilemma further by alternately approaching and avoiding her counselor. She often broke her regular appointments and demanded appointments on an irregular, emergency basis instead. Her intent seemed to be to try to force her counselor to attend to her needs rather than his own. She also alternated between feeling mature and dependent and demanding. In such a case as Miss Mary's, the counselor needs for immediate and continuing gratification border on narcissism rather than nurturance. Said another way, this counselor needed immediate and direct approbation rather than being able to wait for the delayed reward of increased maturity in the client.

Clients who are growing and changing and who may be near termination may also precipitate counselors into sometimes undoing their own work. Since counseling relationships are and should be rewarding to both participants, either member, when termination approaches, may attempt to prolong the relationship by returning it to an earlier more regressed stage. The counselor's behavior, in such an instance, sometimes suggests that he believes he may never have another rewarding relationship. The agonizing distinction between premature termination and needless prolonging is particularly a problem every counselor faces in cases where the encounter has had positive meaning.

Counselor conflicts about adequacy may also result in effecting client regression out of counselor need. Feelings of adequacy are often naturally associated with feelings of need for power. Threats to his adequacy as a counselor, or as a person even, may cause a counselor to attempt regression in a client to reassure himself about his own potency. Such counselor efforts are often revealed by blatant premature interpretations of the client's feelings and behavior. It is as though the counselor is saying, "See how intelligent and perceptive I am." Adequacy in any counseling relationship, we believe, is usually earned by being adequate over a period of time.

When clients express alternating conflicted ambivalent feelings, response to either side of the ambivalence may be revealing of counselor intent to induce regression in the client. The aspect of the ambivalence which is responded to may also tell us something about the counselor's needs and conflicts. For example, a client may express hate and anger as well as a need to have a better relationship with a particular parent. Further exploration and expansion of either kind of feelings will almost certainly lead to further client regression, but for different counselor reasons. Consistent counselor response to and reinforcement of the angry feelings may be more meaningful in relation to the counselor's own angry feelings than to the client's.

In the instance of the ambivalent expression of mixed, conflicted feelings, we believe it is ordinarily most appropriate for the counselor to respond to the feelings as mixed or conflicted. Since the expression of ambivalent feelings tends to be alternating and temporal, the client may not even recognize that he has both kinds of feelings and that they are in conflict. Responding to and clarifying both feelings will often enable the client to go ahead and expand that aspect of the ambivalence which is most significant to him.

However, the counselor should keep in mind that the client's choice may also have defensive value. For example, in the case of Mr. Jerry, the counselor did sensitively recognize the client's angry feelings as well as his need to have a better relationship with his father. The client was startled and yet could not immediately deny the reality of either set of feelings since both were conscious. The client soon chose, however, to go ahead with expanding and expressing his angry feelings. The counselor then seemed to forget, perhaps because of the power of the feelings, that the client had expressed a need for his father. Through a number of interviews, the principal content was an angry ventilation, with support from the counselor, of feelings about the father.

The client eventually developed an emotional cycle consisting of anger, withdrawal, and depression. The relationship was terminated by the client by first breaking appointments and then finally telephoning to break off further contacts in a distant, hostile, disappointed way. In this case, the counselor should perhaps have proceeded initially as he did. Yet his failure to retain and remember the other set of client feelings may have forced the client to attempt to resolve his conflict by breaking off his relationship with both counselor and father.

It is frequently true, we think, that angry feelings can operate to conceal or defend against prior feelings of hurt or deprivation. The counselor began well; but perhaps because of his own conflicts about deprivation, he was unable to see the eventual defensive meaning of the client's anger. Thus the client was never able to expand, know, and reexperience his hurt and thus to find ways to relate satisfactorily to his father.

It is worth noting that the order in which ambivalent, conflicted, or contradictory feelings are expressed may be significant. The feelings which are first expressed may have the most defensive value. In the case just cited, we can conjecture that the client first experienced hurt and that his needs were not being adequately met by his father. Later, since his needs and demands for affection may have been frustrated, he developed angry feelings which defended against feelings of deprivation and also, perhaps, at least enabled him to have an angry relationship with his father. In the initial interview, this client expressed angry feelings first and then his more needful feelings—the reverse of the order in which they probably occurred in his life. This client's counseling experience, then, may have recapitulated his relationship with his father but probably did little to correct or change the relationship.

In summary, we think of regression as a frequent, and perhaps necessary, experience in counseling relationships. The degree and kind of regression, we believe, should ideally be dictated by the client's needs to explore those feelings and experiences which will enable him to change. However, counselor conflicts, needs, dynamics, and misperceptions of client problems may often act to hinder or destroy an effective counseling process. But, again, if the counselor can recognize and understand the consequences of his own behavior before a relationship is destroyed, he can turn mistake into success.

INSIGHT: A DEFENSE AGAINST AFFECT?

In our culture there is increasing emphasis on the need to understand, to predict, and to control the phenomena of nature. An increasing number of books and articles, both popular and scientific, are being written both to rouse and allay anxiety about the complexity or predictability of human behavior as well. This book is, of course, one such effort. We wish to emphasize, in part, that while understanding of any phenomenon necessarily involves an intellectual component, the very drive to understand intellectually may lead us to ignore or defend against the affective base such understanding must have. In our view, as many others have also said, man is an emotional as well as an intellectual animal. We believe understanding of human beings necessarily involves awareness and deep respect for both kinds of strivings and their complex interwoven nature.

Insight, as it may manifest itself in counseling relationships, can be a complex phenomenon which may not always be what it seems. What are the emotional and intellectual concomitants of insight? Or is it entirely intellectual? Or could it be that it is a phenomenon which may not involve consciousness and the cerebral cortex at all? Does insight precede change in human behavior? Or does it follow after affective turmoil and conflict? Probably no one of us has satisfactory or complete answers to any one of these questions, but even though we can claim only partial understandings, these may still be of value.

How does insight occur in counseling relationships? One compelling argument is that insight precedes reorganization. Here the idea is that, as is often true of things in the physical world, the object, piece of machinery, or whatever is understood in terms of intellectual comprehension. Such a way of viewing the physical and natural world as well as mankind has much utility. Much of scientific method and investigation hinges its success on the ability to conceptualize possible cause and effect relationships, to synthesize prior data and findings, and to formulate further hypotheses for testing. Such a view has meaning for counseling relationships as well as more strictly scientific investigation. In many ways the procedures just described fit the diagnostic workings of the counselor as he endeavors to activate an effective counseling relationship and struggles to understand and resolve an impasse he and his client have reached. Yet, on the other hand, as accounts in literature attest, many significant "hunches" about the nature of the world have come to the discoverer suddenly, without much prior thought, and with a sense of internal reorganization which is reported affectively.

We offer, then, the proposition that often understanding, discovering, or changing any phenomenon involves an affective component. Such understanding or discovery is often preceded by an apparent decrease in intellectual effort and an increase in affective ferment. Our own experience in doing the research which led to this book often involved such an intellectual-affective switch. Our writing, too, has been both facilitated and hindered by the same kind of cyclic experiences.

Our own experience as counselors and our understanding of how others function in the counseling relationship lead us to say that both affective and cognitive dimensions enter into an effective counseling process. However, we wish also to emphasize that we think it is rare that significant changes in human behavior occur without an affective experience. Change in behavior in regard to other humans, the interpersonal dimension, as we understand it, almost invariably calls for an affective, and often, conflicted experience.

We can answer some of our earlier questions by saying that insight or adequate conceptualization can precede change. But often the most significant conceptions occur after an emotional experience and are often accompanied by a deep sense of internal reorganization and change.

That purely intellectual understanding unaccompanied by a corrective emotional experience in relationship to another person is often ineffective is illustrated by the intelligent, introspective client. Such clients are often highly accurate, as later events often prove, about the nature of their problems and even about the origins of their difficulties. Yet these clients still speak of themselves as deeply dissatisfied with the changes they have made and with the rewards that accrue to them from the external world. The same clients, after an emotionally disrupting experience such as counseling may be, will report with conviction years later that their lives have changed for the better. Sometimes our less than perfect measuring devices may even reflect such change.

Client needs to utilize their insights about themselves and others may effect counseling relationships in various ways. In one instance, a client's apparently clear and unconflicted perceptions of himself may lead his counselor to believe the client has no problems worth attention. What the counselor may miss is that this apparently clear view is defensive and intended, in part, to avoid the painful affective interpersonal encounters which may genuinely change him.

In another case, if the counselor can understand that the client's insights may have defensive value, then the counselor may be able to "discount" appropriately and move ahead to assist the client in expanding his conflicts and feelings. Such a distinction can be very difficult to make, however, and can often be seen and understood only after the counseling relationship has developed. It may prove to be quite disturbing to the client's well-organized defense.

Insight or conceptualization by the counselor can also be helpful or hindering to his efforts to help clients. As we have suggested earlier, counselor insights involving generic diagnoses may be most useful in initiating a counseling relationship. But such diagnoses may be a convenient defense for the counselor to retreat to when powerful affective storms are unleashed by his client. An initial conceptualization of a client's problems which is not being constantly modified, changed, and enriched by the ongoing relationship suggests that the relationship is in danger of being ineffective. Counselors may invoke and utilize insight or diagnostic skill when their own adequacy is threatened. At such times a counselor may attempt to recoup his potency by a barrage of more or less acute observations about his client and his behavior. Clients may even accept or comply with some of the observations. We suspect, however, that the client may often be accepting only to preserve and continue the relationship for its possible therapeutic value. The counselor's insights may only reveal him to the client.

Insight, as we define it, has both affective and cognitive dimensions. Both aspects operate continuously in a complex way in the counseling relationship. It may sometimes facilitate change, and yet, often the most significant experience of insight occurs after an emotional upheaval has occurred. We add, too, that the counselor may find himself most emotionally touched, even awed, when he and his client finally may understand what they have been through together.

THE DOUBLE-EDGED SWORD OF BEING ADEQUATE

Adequacy is the counselor's passport to unraveling his client's conflicts and effecting change. But adequacy is a double-edged sword and it can easily shade into omnipotence on the one hand and impotence on the other hand. The counselor's adequacy will most assuredly activate the client's conflicts, and the client's conflicted feelings in turn will trigger a wish to immobilize the counselor in order to keep from changing. Since the client's present situation, although discomforting, is more comfortable than the prospect of exploring the unknown, he will become hypersensitive to chinks in the armor of the counselor's adequacy. In this respect, the counselor's adequacy makes him vulnerable to attack as the client searches for ways of maintaining his old emotional state and attempts to keep from changing.

The challenge to the counselor's adequacy may also stem from his own internal conflicts. When the counselor becomes most adequate with the client and activates the client's conflicts, he may himself experience some fears regarding the extent and depth of his own adequacy. These fears may arise from his feelings of omnipotence that crowd in on him as he realizes his ability to profoundly influence another human being. The threat to the counselor's adequacy, therefore, may activate in him some need to reduce the intensity of the relationship to prevent his own anxiety from overwhelming him. Whereas the need to reduce the intensity of the relationship arises in the client from his fears about what it will mean to change, the counselor's fears are aroused when he observes the effects of his stimulation on the client.

The counselor's own past conflicts may be reactivated at points when his adequacy is stirring up feelings about his potency and when his client is reacting against his potency. The consequences of his inner experiences and the experiences that are provoked by the client may be sufficient to cause the counselor to hesitate and distrust his own motivation and effectiveness. Earlier we spoke of a counselor whose own inner experiences regarding the strength of his influence on the client and what he was recreating in the client caused him to question his motivation. We will take a moment to reexamine that case since it represents how a counselor's ambivalence can be activated by his own adequacy.

In the case of Miss Paula the counselor's effectiveness at once activated his client's conflicts and his own feelings of omnipotence. The counselor's concern about being omnipotent took emotional precedence over his regard for his client, and the consequences of his abdicating his position of strength were terrifying to the client. The reader will recall that in that particular case it was the counselor's strength and competence which permitted the client to reexperience painful feelings from her own past. The counselor's abdication of strength served to incapacitate the client and she reverted to attempting frantically to reactivate old defenses. The critical incident occurred because the counselor abdicated his responsibility by withdrawing his protection from the client after he had created the conditions which were guaranteed to facilitate the client's regression. Unfortunately, the client's defenses had been perforated by the promise of strength and she had less to fall back on to remobilize herself than before counseling.

Even though the counselor became frightened by his own omnipotence, the case also reflects our belief that these incidents, although they may be therapeutic errors and may jeopardize the relationship, are revocable. In this case the errors were corrected in such a way that the counselor not only reestablished his strength and was able to continue to work with the client, but he had also learned something of the client's response to inconsistency in significant persons. The threat to the client's safety in this case stemmed from the counselor's withdrawing his strength because his own conflicted feelings interfered with his counseling.

The opposite side of the coin also obtains when the client experiences the counselor's adequacy as a threat to him and when he actively tries to immobilize the counselor to reduce the threat. In these cases, it is the client who, out of his own need to defend against change, attempts to utilize a number of events in the relationship in order to reduce the counselor's effectiveness. Such a client may tongue-lash the counselor and, as in one of the cases we presented earlier, attempt to convince the counselor that he is in a worse state as a result of having seen this counselor and having worked with him.

If the counselor does not recognize that the intensity of the relationship, the client's heightened anxiety, and his ambivalence about changing have activated his anger, then the counselor may attempt to placate the client, to reassure him, to readjust his sights, to reduce his own effectiveness, or to somehow inadvertently undo what he has achieved.

If the counselor's reasons for reevaluating his goals with this client are motivated by such desires as keeping the relationship smooth, avoiding a client's anger, quieting troubled waters, they are generally inappropriate or insufficient motives for changing objectives. We assume that the counselor should have made a series of continuing judgments about the strength of the client and his ability to tolerate the anxiety necessary to change; so we wonder whether responding to the client's heightened anxiety—which is an essential precursor to change—by attempting to reduce it is an appropriate counseling move. It would rather seem that the counselor's adequacy has been threatened, and his own anxiety has so clouded the picture that he is unable to evaluate adequately the tone of the relationship.

How susceptible a counselor is to readjusting his goals because of the anxiety that he experiences as a result of the client's demands on him or his own inner experiences of fear about the potent effects of his behavior on the client will be a function, of course, of the counselor's dynamics and conflicts. A counselor's dynamics may be such that he needs to be liked or to have some immediate approbation for his behavior with a client in order for him to continue to be effective with that client. Any threat to that approbation may then be disabling to the counselor, and a client's anger expressed directly and openly toward him may precipitate his behaving irrationally with the client. What such a counselor experiences in the client's anger is the potential threat of the client withdrawing his love and affection for the counselor whenever the counselor behaves in the ways he must behave in order to effect change in the client.

Such counselor behavior must certainly be reminiscent to the client of his past experiences with other significant persons. The client may have successfully manipulated his parents into relinquishing their responsibility on the similar grounds that they were being hurtful or cruel to him because of their demands on him. By convincing his parents that they were behaving inappropriately with him, the child may have avoided any kind of threatening experience. His parents, in effect, may have been talked out of assisting their child to meet and handle the usual developmental tasks. At these critical times in his development, the parents probably felt some concern about their behavior toward the child and questioned their own motivations rather than the motivation of the child.

In his current relationship with that same person, the counselor has responded in the same way by examining his own motivation rather than questioning the motivation of the client. We would think that when a counselor's own need for nurturance and approval from a client is so strong that he satisfies it at the expense of the client's needs, the counselor is probably not having his own needs met satisfactorily in his other relationships. The counselor may profitably reevaluate why his emotional needs are so intense that he compromises his own effectiveness and everything his training has taught him in order to have them satisfied by a client.

The counselor's need for approval or affection is but one reason why a client's anger may affect a counselor so strongly. The counselor's own past experiences may have been such that he feels that his strength hangs in the balance of whims of the persons who are important to him. These fears of being rendered impotent by clients may become particularly incapacitating. Such counseling relationships often reflect the inability of the counselor to experience his adequacy as something that is his independent of the client's feelings about whether he is adequate.

If the counselor is so constituted that he believes that his adequacy is the function of other people giving it to him or taking it away, then how he behaves in a given relationship will be determined by the ephemeral needs, demands, and opinions of his client. When a counselor's adequacy is a function of the client's willingness to give it to him, then at those points where the counselor is behaving adequately and the threat of change is intense, the client to protect himself will attempt to take away that adequacy again. If the sequence of events were tracked in relationships where the counselor bargains for his adequacy, we could probably discern times early in that relationship when the client was the one who gave the counselor his adequacy.

How can a client give a counselor his adequacy? For one thing, he can only give it to the counselor if, as we have stated above, the counselor supports the myth that his feelings of adequacy are contingent on the volition of others. And clients will often reinforce this fiction for they too sometimes feel that they have the strength to give and to take away adequacy. We often see clients whose emotional development indicates that they were reared in a home atmosphere where the parents demanded that the child nurture the parents rather than that the parents nurture the child. In such an atmosphere, the child learns that how he feels matters only if he can satisfy in a prior way his parents' needs. But a child may also learn that not only are his needs secondary but that when he refrains from nurturing his parents, they are emotionally threatened. Developmentally, the client has learned from this sequence of events with his parents that he controls in an emotional sense how the parents feel.

We have noted that clients attempt to make counselors feel good by telling them repeatedly that they are doing a good job. Whether the client says this to the counselor is not the important thing. The important thing for our consideration here is the strength of the client's belief that he controls the counselor's adequacy which may mesh with the counselor's needs to have the client tell him he is adequate so that he can feel good about this counseling. If this is the state of affairs, then it would seem that the counselor's adequacy is truly a function of whether or not this client is willing to give it to him. The resulting relationship in such a situation may well be non-therapeutic.

The counselor's adequacy may also flow into feelings of omnipotence as we said earlier. These feelings are inner feelings which are within the counselor and they may not have so much to do with this particular client as they have to do with this counselor's general attitude toward persons and his relationships with them. A counselor who is easily stirred to feeling omnipotent in his relationships may wonder what motivates him in his relationships to be adequate. It may well be that a counselor's adequacy in the relationship arises out of his need to be omnipotent and such motivation is usually not very therapeutic unless it is recognized and understood. That is, the counselor's gratification flows from the feeling that he strongly influences the behavior of other people rather than from the fact that the influence that he has on other people can be of help to them in changing because they want and need to change in order to get along more comfortably.

Such a counselor may become immobilized when the impact of his motivations strike him. His own motivations will begin to seep through into consciousness at points where his influence is strong and his feelings will become intense and frightening and he may attempt to draw back. In the case of Miss Paula, the fact that the counselor did draw back in his relationship with that client indicates something of the intensity of the feelings that he was experiencing; his willingness to reduce his own anxiety at the expense of the client also reveals something of the mixed motivation that stimulated him to be adequate in the first place.

Counselor adequacy always has a temporal dimension. This is true in the sense that the counselor's ability to help may be questioned by either counselor or client at any point during a given relationship. Perhaps adequacy may only be finally established when change has occurred and the relationship is terminated. As a consequence of the constant and continuing question, anxiety is likely to be present in both participants until the question is resolved by success, failure, or impasse. The counselor's constant and continuing anxiety about his adequacy can be adaptive or destructive depending on his own conflicts and the nature of his interaction with his client. On the one hand, if the counselor can accept and believe that the proof of his adequacy must necessarily be long delayed, then he can frequently utilize the stimulus of his own anxiety to assist him in understanding the course of his relationships with his clients. Particularly at times when the ever-present anxiety flares in its intensity, he can know that something may be amiss which calls for better understanding. At such periods, if the counselor can avoid becoming either immobilized or too reactive, he can frequently follow the course of his own anxiety and arrive at a deeper personal awareness and consequently be of more help to his client.

On the other hand, if a counselor has little tolerance for the constant experience of anxiety, he may be led to engage in behaviors which reduce his anxiety at the expense of his client. Such anxiety reducing may take the form of seeking unearned approbation from his client, self-recriminations, angry projections about the client's recalcitrance, or premature termination. Anxiety about one's adequacy as a counselor, then, can be turned to adaptive and constructive uses, or it can be used to destroy when the adequacy is too desperately sought.

Adequacy as a counselor is temporal in another sense. We observe that past success with one or many clients does not automatically assure success with any given client in the present. While it is true that past successes may enable a counselor to enter a present relationship with some feelings of adequacy and expectations that he can help this person, his final adequacy must be earned by being adequate over a period of time with this particular client. Successful past experience may help a counselor to have generalized feelings of competence, but the fact that this adequacy must continually be earned again leads to an enduring humility about particular relationships.

THE PROCESS OF SUPERVISION:

Facilitating Counseling Relationships

CONTROL AND FACILITATION:
Complementary Processes of Supervision

Chapter 5

The control of the behavior of other human beings is a matter of concern in many stages and aspects of human life and development. Parents are usually deeply involved in both the control and facilitation of their children's growth. Schools and other institutions preoccupy themselves with the same issues. Business men want their employees to be both productive and satisfied with their lives in the world of work. Government wishes the citizens of the country to be productive, perhaps even creative, as human beings; yet there is also concern that the people be well behaved and law-abiding.

Control of others and the facilitation of growth and development can be viewed as conflicting or contradictory processes. Statements are often made, too, that the processes are not antithetical; but the behavior of the controller suggests that internally he views the processes as not complementary. On the one hand, the person with control prerogatives may say, "I want you to grow and develop." Yet the same person behaves in ways which block or impede the development of those for whom he has some responsibility. We can all recognize the double message of the father who says that his college age son is "completely free" to choose any occupation as long as he chooses the "right" one. How can anyone have any freedom to choose if he is also enjoined that he must be right the first time he chooses?

We may also recognize the contradictory intents of the teacher who tells his students, often vehemently, that they should be "honest" and "say what they think." Yet this same teacher is often punitive verbally and behaviorally and may fail the student for speaking or writing honestly what he feels and thinks. Choice anxiety is made of such stuff! Students, employees, and perhaps, children most of all, are often highly cognizant of such double messages. The degree to which any given individual can cope adequately with the many contradictory messages which flood in from the world is, of course, a function of his past life with all of its conflicts, impasses, and resolutions. To some extent, a person's coping ability can be assessed by the kinds of double messages he recognizes and how he deals with them.

It is probably true that, in our human imperfection, each of us gives messages with contradictory intent to others with whom we interact. However, it is our belief that, if recognized, such communications can be changed or corrected. Perhaps the significant human difference between controllers who are viewed positively as compared with those who are not lies in the willingness and ability of some persons to recognize and modify their own contradictory communications to others.

From our point of view, then, many human problems arise because control of others and facilitation of growth, creativity, and change in others are often dynamically dealt with as contradictory or incompatible. We also believe, however, that the processes of control and growth can be dynamically seen and dealt with as complementary. That this is feasible is attested to by the fact that at least a significant minority of adults are socially acceptable, behaviorally controlled, and yet they can also be spontaneous and creative in thought and action.

Supervision of others, wherever it may occur, can be a process of control and inhibition without compensating freedom. Or, we maintain, it can be a process which provides needed control and complementary support for exploration, creativity, development, and change. The adult, perhaps less clearly and vividly than does the child, has needs both for control and for spontaneous, free expression. Since these needs may be experienced as incompatible, usually because of earlier training which reinforced contradiction rather than blending or joining, supervision may be viewed by the supervisor as inhibition of those he supervises. Or, those supervised may react as though conformity or rebellion are the only choices.

As we have indicated, none of these alternatives is necessarily true. The good supervisor, we believe, combines in his own person those qualities which cause others to believe that he can control, if necessary, and also that he is emotionally supportive of exploration, experimentation, and learning for its own sake. Further, the good supervisor does not ordinarily experience these qualities in himself as being emotionally competitive or antithetical. Supervision, in one sense, involves a complex, yet understandable, interpersonal expression of qualities which enhance feelings of trust and security and at the same time allows those being supervised the freedom to learn, grow, and change.

The reader may wonder at this point whether good supervisors are born or made. In reply, we say that a fortunate choice of parents and a reasonably good hurdling of the developmental tasks of growing up are most helpful. However, we also believe that supervisors, as is true of counselors and clients, can learn, change, and develop qualities which they may be initially lacking. Such learning and changing can be anxiety rousing but most rewarding.

Supervision of Counselors: an enabling
process

Our general theory about the nature of supervision emphasizes the compatibility of control and facilitation. Supervision and training of counselors call imperatively for integration of these functions in a complex and subtle way. We propose that the supervisory relationship is another instance of a significant interpersonal relationship which shares many similarities to a counseling relationship. Counselor conflicts and dynamics are likely to surface in supervision. Supervisor attitudes, helpful and otherwise, will become evident. The complex interaction of counselor and supervisor attitudes, conflicts, and dynamics will determine whether the supervisory

relationship is helpful and facilitating or inhibiting and destructive
of counselor growth and development.

Counselors-in-training, or even independently functioning experienced persons, may approach a supervisory relationship as
though the supervisor should take over, control, and manage the
counselor's relationships to his clients. If such a state of affairs
actually comes to pass and continues for any extended period of
time, then the relationship has produced inhibiting control but not
growth and expansion of counselor capability. Interestingly enough,
such a supervisory relationship often comes to be regarded by the
counselor as punitive, unhelpful, and destructive. He may even
avoid the relationship which his own behavior helped to create.

The principal point here is that the counselor has elicited
control from the supervisor much as the counselor's own clients
may be eliciting control from him. The counselor cannot change
his own behavior with his clients since he has a similar parallel
reinforcing relationship with his supervisor. We suggest that a
counselor may often attempt to create a relationship with his supervisor which is similar in some significant dimensions to the relationships he has with his clients. The supervisory relationship
then may serve as a defensive screen which enables the counselor
to continue, and even justify, the unchanging, probably ineffective ways he is treating his clients. Concurrently, the counselor may
express continuing feelings of dissatisfaction and impotence.

For what reasons does a supervisor permit, or even encourage,
a supervisory relationship which reinforces inhibition, invariance,
and consequent lack of growth in a counselor? The reasons for
such supervisor behavior are undoubtedly complex, subtle, and
varied. One primary motivation, expressed in a number of variations, has emerged as most significant to explain such supervisor
control. The first of these variations is that the supervisor has needs
to believe that the counselor cannot find, even with the supervisor's
help, personal resources which reside within the counselor. Another
supervisor control behavior involves fears that the counselor may,
in fact, be effective and perhaps not need the supervisor's help.
Or, it may be feared that the counselor might be or will become
as effective a counselor, perhaps even better, than is the supervisor himself.

All these variations in feelings and consequent behaviors probably reflect the supervisor's uneasy feelings about himself professionally and as a person. Since the supervisor may then suffer from severe doubts about his own adequacy, he may often not permit or facilitate the adequacy of others, or, if he does it will be on a limited basis. That is, the supervisor can tolerate counselor growth to a certain point. When this limit is reached, the threat causes the supervisor to invoke controls and restrictions.

One effect of the supervisor behaviors and feelings just described is to limit counselor development. Also, however, since the effect of the behaviors is ultimately belittling to the counselor, the supervisor's behavior, if long continued, will cause the counselor to feel punished as well. The counselor will, depending on his own dynamic response to punishment, become further constricted and invariant or he may rebel and attempt to establish his independence by fighting with the supervisor or even avoiding the supervisory relationship.

No supervisor is invulnerable to threat from those he supervises. Nor should he be; for it is often through the very threat that is posed that the supervisor can become aware of his own feelings and what may have occurred in the supervisory relationship. A supervisor who can recognize being threatened and go ahead to differentiate his own feelings can usually restore supervision's usefulness. Further, as a supervisor is able to differentiate himself from those he supervises, so he will also be able to assist his supervisees to differentiate themselves from their clients.

DIFFERENTIATION AND CHANGE

The clients who enter a counseling relationship almost universally enter with mixed fears and wishes about what the process of changing will be like. On the one hand, the client tries to convey the feeling that his problems are complicated, that they are difficult to understand, and that their resolution will require some investment on the counselor's part. The client believes that he must convince the counselor that working with him will be rewarding, that his problems are challenging, and that he is an intriguing person.

Equally clear when he enters counseling are the client's fears, expressed in numerous ways: that he is afraid to change; that he is threatened by the loss of his own identity in the process; and that he is distrustful of how the counselor will use his perceptiveness.

These mixed fears and wishes dynamically determine the expression of the clients' feelings at a number of levels. The fact is, of course, that the client's problems are complicated. When his basic needs have not been met directly in the past, the client has learned to set into operation an intricate set of devices with subtly constructed checks and balances so that he can satisfy his needs in indirect and circuitous ways. Depending upon how threatening the environment has been, the intensity of the wish for the desired responses from others increases as the needs go unmet and yet, paradoxically, the alarm system of approaching danger to having his underlying feelings and needs discovered becomes increasingly intricate.

The wish for help and the fear of change may be counterbalanced when the client enters counseling. What guarantee does the client have that he will not be punished if he is expressive of what he feels and that as a consequence of his self-revelations he will subsequently need to find new, even more secretive, ways of achieving satisfaction? In addition, the client must also wonder whether the construction of new ways of coping with his environment will be as good as or better than the current modes of satisfying his needs. The client's concern about what the search for alleviation of his discomfort may mean to his emotional life is the basic substratum on which the client's ambivalence about committing himself to counseling is constructed.

But, there is still another way of looking at the meaning of the client's fears and wishes. Often when a client enters counseling he has compressed or choked off the affect that was associated with significant events in his life. In its compressed and encapsulated form, the client's feelings are available to him for change only in a gross form. The client may experience his environment and everyone in it in a highly undifferentiated way. The client may believe that counselors are "good," that he is "bad," and that his parents are "ideal" or "destructive." The client is unable to discriminate between how his father responds to him as compared to his mother, how their responses to each other differ from their responses to him, or how their personalities may be mixtures of characteristics that the client likes and dislikes. When the client's feelings and anticipations of others' responses are so amorphous, when his affect is experienced in such an either-or state, when his attitudes are packaged in such an indiscriminating way, when the client's environment is so undifferentiated, change is terrifying because of the consequent threat of loss of identity.

The Supervisor: a differentiating person

Just as the client's undifferentiated experiences make change difficult for him, so also is it difficult for a counselor to help his clients to be more differentiating and thereby to change unless the counselor views his environment and his own relationships in highly differentiated ways. Supervision is one source of assistance that the counselor can utilize to facilitate his counseling relationships and thus become a more differentiating person. One of the ways in which the supervisor enables the counselor to counsel is by helping the counselor to differentiate his own feelings and conflicts from those of the client.

The enabling process also means that the supervisor is able to differentiate his understanding of human behavior, his counseling skills, and his feelings from those of the counselor that he is supervising. The supervisor generally has more professional experience and training than the counselor that he is supervising. His own experiences may mean that if he were the counselor he would behave in particular ways with his supervisee's clients, and the ways in which the supervisor would behave and the goals that he would set may in fact be different from the ways that his supervisee anticipates the process and goals.

There are several supervisory alternatives to reconciling the differences between the supervisor's and his supervisee's approach to their counseling relationships and the objectives they hope to achieve. The supervisor can expect, for example, that the counselor with whom he is working will set the objectives that the supervisor would establish and will behave in the counseling relationship as the supervisor himself would behave. Alternatively, the supervisor may work with his supervisee to develop, understand, and achieve objectives that seem appropriate to the supervisee even though these objectives may be different from those that he himself would set. In the same way that all significant human relationships have consequences in terms of the participants' eventual feelings of adequacy, so, too, the supervisory relationships that develop from either of these premises will have a continuing impact on both persons and may eventuate in growth and productivity or a significant failure for counselor and supervisor alike.

A Supervisory Premise: management from afar

Supervision which assumes that the supervisor's superior knowledge of human behavior should dictate the nature of the process and objectives that his supervisee establishes suggests a number of consequences. Since the objectives are the supervisor's, the weight of the responsibility for achieving the objectives must also lie with the supervisor. When the supervisor establishes the objectives, he assumes the burden of proof; and the supervisory relationship becomes a process of management from afar as the supervisor attempts to control the ensuing counseling relationship indirectly.

Based on the premise of vicarious control, supervision shifts responsibility for what occurs in the relationship from the counselor to the supervisor. Freed of his responsibility for the consequences of his behavior with the client, the counselor becomes something of a robot. His freedom from responsibility may have been purchased at the price of being effective, however, because it is in the process of the counselor's committing himself to the client and assuming his share of responsibility for the ensuing exploration under reciprocal stress that therapeutic change is more likely to occur.

When the supervisor assumes responsibility for establishing the counseling objectives and dictates the process, he may take the stress out of the relationship for the counselor; but he may also remove the counselor's strength as well. Stripped of his resources, the counselor's effectiveness with his client is nullified since, as a technician, his human resources have been taken away from him. Such supervisory relationships have been reduced to the "button-button" game where the supervisor, counselor, and client are engaged in searching for "who's got the adequacy."

Actually, of course, when a supervisory relationship has so developed, the supervisor's own adequacy has been placed in the hands of the counselor. When the supervisor assumes the responsibility for counseling objectives, he is forced to attempt to implement his objectives through the counselor. Paradoxically, the proof of the supervisor's adequacy now hinges on the counselor's behaving in the prescribed ways with his client; yet by setting his objectives beyond the scope of the counselor's understanding, the supervisor may have little hope of achieving his objectives.

The supervisor's motivation for establishing the counseling objectives and suggesting the process by which these goals are to be reached is usually mixed. On the one hand, the supervisor may actually have strong convictions about how to work with a client who manifests the particular behavioral problems of his supervisee's client, and he may have actually experienced change in clients like this one when he approached them in certain ways. His own anxiety, therefore, about what the counselor and client will achieve in their relationship may lead him to impose objectives. So part of his motivation is the wish to be helpful.

But the motivation is mixed; for although he wishes to be helpful to one human being, the supervisor achieves his goals at the expense of another person. That the supervisor would bypass the feelings of the supervisee is perhaps also revealing of other factors about his need to control which motivates him to establish such a supervisory relationship. Lastly, the supervisor's anxiety which activates his need to control may be a reflection of the supervisor's own conflicts about his adequacy. And, since the supervisor's adequacy is contingent on his supervisee's behaving according to prescription, his feelings about the supervisee will fluctuate according to the supervisee's success.

The supervisor's feelings about his supervisee are likely to be complicated further if the source of his own conflicted feelings stems from concerns about male adequacy. The supervisor may be disturbed by his own behavior which has incapacitated the counselor and he may attempt to ward off his own fears of being incapacitated in turn by punishing the counselor for being weak.

The consequences of the supervisor's attempt to use the counselor as the instrument for achieving his own objectives with clients
are conflict-laden for the counselor as well. On the one hand, the
counselor may begin to feel angry with the supervisor for attempting to control and manipulate his clients. Yet, his wishes to manage his own affairs and accept the consequences for his own behavior may be countered by fears that the supervisor may punish
him if he is unsuccessful in his attempts to govern his own client
relationships. Caught between the wish to regain his adequacy
and his fears of further professional impoverishment, the counselor's
frustration will probably be experienced in angry feelings toward
the supervisor.

But even these angry feelings may be displaced onto the client
because the counselor's adequacy is in the hands of his supervisor,
and the counselor still wishes to be rewarded and evaluated highly
by the supervisor for behaving according to the supervisor's wishes.
In the same way that the threat to the supervisor's adequacy stimulated his becoming angry with the counselor when he was not effective, so the counselor, whose adequacy is also at stake, may become
angry with the client when he does not behave in accordance with
the supervisor's predictions.

The counselor's wish to be rewarded, his fear of being punished, his frustrations about his own adequacy, and his wishes to
express his own independence must take their toll on the client. The
client probably experiences the counseling relationship in confused
ways. The supervisor's understanding of the client's dynamics is
often accurate and his overseeing of the counseling process may pay
off in that the counselor brings a technical know-how to sessions
that he has gathered from his recent supervisory sessions. But these
client understandings are probably short-lived since they are based
on a cookbook approach and since they are mixed with the counselor's own confused feelings about himself and the client.

The counselor's feelings toward the client are probably reminiscent of the supervisor's feelings about the counselor. As such,
the counselor may experience the client as an instrument or an
obstacle to his professional development and his regard for the
client may be secondary to his wish to satisfy the supervisor. When
the counselor's adequacy is torn away, with it may go his personal

involvement with and feelings of responsibility toward the client. These feelings of involvement and responsibility are the bases of counseling relationships. It is because the counselor has committed himself to help the client that he feels anxiety about the meaning of the client's words and affect; that he is sensitive to what under-lies the expressed words and behavior of the client, and that he is able to predict accurately how his client will behave between ses-sions and what his behavior means.

The supervisor's attempt to manage the relationship from afar damages the supervisor's adequacy and potential growth as well as that of the counselor he supervises and the clients that his super-visee counsels. Once the supervisory relationships get caught up in the "adequacy-adequacy—who's got the adequacy" game, every-one loses. When the myth is accepted and perpetuated that there is but one "button" of adequacy, the players lose sight of their wish to help and their humanness is replaced with a struggle to locate and regain their fantasied loss of strength.

A Supervisory Premise: facilitating the counselor's relationships

A supervisory relationship may develop in which the supervisor assumes the posture that his task is to help his supervisee facili-tate the objectives and process that the supervisee wishes to imple-ment, even though the ensuing counseling relationships and objec-tives may be different from those of the supervisor. Such a position is posited on the belief that there may be no "best" way in which someone can change, but rather that a person's feelings and ulti-mately his behavior may change as a result of the impact of a significant interaction with another human being and that these interactions may be of many different kinds. The basic premise of this supervisory position is that potential client change may accrue from contact with counselors whose orientations toward how change occurs, whose personalities, and whose counseling objec-tives may be quite different from each other.

We think that persons change and grow—clients or counselors —when they experience a relationship that evinces a concern for their resources and for their feelings. In the supervisory relationship, the counselor is as vulnerable to hurt and can experience the damaging consequences of a significant failure in the same way that a client often does. Counseling is, after all, just the professional embodiment of the counselor's personal needs to achieve, to be recognized, and to be deemed an adequate person. How effective he can be with his own clients is related in no small way to how satisfactorily the counselor's own needs are met in the supervisory relationship. The supervisor who respects the counselor as a person will establish the kind of relationship with him in which he can change and grow.

In some respects, the supervisory relationship parallels the counseling relationship—it can not be free of stress nor should it be so anxiety-laden that the counselor spends his supervisory time in struggling to reduce his anxiety rather than being free to use his anxiety to understand better his feelings about his clients. On the other hand, when the supervisory relationship is free of stress, it may reflect the same state of affairs that we described earlier when the supervisor attempted to manage his supervisee's relationships. A supervisory relationship that is free of stress is one which is contemptuous of the counselor's strength and does not extend the counselor so that he can grow maximally.

Alternatively, a supervisory relationship in which the tension is incapacitating to the counselor reflects the fact that the supervisor's own needs have become more important than his regard for the growth of the counselor. A supervisor who induces excessive anxiety into the counselor's relationships with his clients under the guise of being helpful may actually need to punish this counselor or to demonstrate his own adequacy. If a supervisor's perceptiveness seriously threatens a counselor's competence, we wonder how useful such an experience can be for the counselor.

Good differentiation is the basis for healthy supervisory relationships. In order to assist his supervisee in his counseling relationships, the supervisor must be sufficiently aware of his own needs and conflicts so that his motivations for his supervising behavior are available to him. Unless the supervisor can track the sequence of events in the supervisory relationship that activated his needs to prove his adequacy or be destructive of the counselor's potential, the supervisory relationship will often deteriorate.

The supervisor must also differentiate his feelings about his supervisee's clients from those of the counselor whom he is supervising. A supervisor needs only to observe the counseling behavior or listen to the recorded interviews of counselors with very different personalities, varying levels of sophistication, and different orientations toward how change occurs to experience some humility about imposing his own objectives or process onto the counseling relationships of his supervisees.

How, then, can the supervisor be helpful to his supervisee? A major emphasis in a supervisory relationship which is based on the principle of facilitating the supervisee's relationships is that of studying the dynamics of the interaction between the client and counselor which are expediting or inhibiting the relationship. In this way, the events in the supervisee's relationships with his clients that activate the supervisee's anxiety and defenses and that precipitate therapeutic impasses serve as one of the major sources of supervisory material. Although the principal sources of stress that the supervisor utilizes to assist the counselor to learn more about himself as a counselor derive from his supervisee's counseling interactions with his clients, the supervisor may sometimes find it necessary to introduce additional stress into supervisory relationships when his supervisee has reached a therapeutic impasse and yet the supervisee's defenses prevent his anxiety from being experienced directly.

Supervision, then, is a process in which the supervisor sensitively uses the stress that has been activated in the counselor as a consequence of his encounters with his clients, or he may introduce additional stress into the relationship so that the counselor can grow professionally. We think that the supervisory relationship becomes significant when the critical incidents that the counselor has introduced into the relationship are explored under stress. At those times in his professional and personal development, the counselor, like his client, is most vulnerable to change and growth.

In their exploration under stress of the dynamic meaning of the counseling interaction, the supervisor has an opportunity of effectively communicating his understanding of human behavior to his supervisee. In this way, the supervisor does not actively tamper with the supervisee's objectives; nor does he assume that he needs to redirect the process. The supervisor who develops a supervisory relationship based on the principle of facilitating the counselor's relationships happily settles for the more rewarding task of helping the counselor to understand better the meaning of his interaction with his clients—his feelings, attitudes, wishes, fears—and of helping the counselor to differentiate himself from the client.

DIFFERENTIATING THE COUNSELOR'S DYNAMICS

Supervisors enable counselors to counsel by helping them to differentiate their feelings and conflicts from those of their clients Counseling, as we have described it, is a special case of human interaction in which both parties reciprocally affect each other and in which the client's changing behavior is contingent on the counselor's awareness of his own experience and impact. Such a concept of counseling implies, and we have elaborated this concept earlier, that the relationship matures and change occurs only when the meaning of the counselor's own behavior is available to him. A client changes, grows, and becomes more human when the counselor is sensitive to the client's resources and lends his competence, strength, and understanding to the client's exploration of his conflicts.

The supervisor, then, is a person, who, through his interaction with the counselor, attempts to assist him to develop, to restore if necessary, and to bring his relationships with his clients to a satisfying close. One of the ways in which the supervisor helps the counselor to develop and restore his counseling relationships stems from the supervisor's understanding of human behavior and the conflicts and comfort which can emanate from significant encounters.

The supervisor brings his understanding of the sources of human conflict to bear on his supervisee's interaction with his clients by helping the counselor differentiate his own feelings and conflicts from those of his client. A counselor can counsel best when his own impact on the client and the client's impact on him is experienced as it is occurring. Only when the counselor is affectively and cognitively in phase with the client and when his own feelings about the relationship and his impact are experienced as his client experiences them can the relationship mature.

Often the only evidence that the counselor has for whether his experiences are genuine is from what his client tells him. And clients do tell their counselors much that is helpful. They do so by beginning to change or by becoming circular, by putting their anxiety to work or by becoming restless and diffusely anxious, by talking of termination, perhaps ambivalently but with purpose, or by taking flight.

Provided that the counselor can use these cues, he may look at his own behavior as the precipitating events of the client's changing feelings or restlessness. But sometimes when the client expresses restlessness or threatens to run from the relationship, the counselor may be so embroiled in the process that he is not able to "see" what he has precipitated. At such critical times, the counselor's anxiety about what is occurring between him and the client often is related to the unavailability to the counselor of his own feelings. The counselor's uneasiness, triggered by stimulation from the client, may be a cause of alarm to him; yet he may not be able to track the meaning of his feelings.

There are many reasons why a counselor's conflicts may become activated and overwhelm and incapacitate him, preventing him from working effectively toward the resolution of the client's problems. The client's words and feelings, his affect and symptoms, may demand behavioral responses from the counselor that he is unable to make because of his own feelings about what it would mean to meet such demands. For change to occur, a client may need to experience certain events or feelings in his relationship with his counselor that the counselor may believe he can not tolerate himself.

The ensuing impasse may result from the fact that the counselor is unable to use his own feelings to further the relationship and his sensitivity to the client's dynamics is blocked. The counselor's wish to help the client to change may be countered by fears about what undergirds the client's problems or by fears that his own impulses may surface in uncontrolled ways. The counselor may imagine, for example, that he will discover his own conflicts under the client's defenses and that the two of them will be in the muddle together. This anxiety may become sufficiently strong so that the counselor can no longer hear the dynamic message in what the client says, and he can only respond to the client at the level of the symptoms. The counselor may even distract the client and precipitate a termination.

To revitalize the counselor's understanding of the client's conflicts and how they are being expressed interpersonally requires that the meaning of the counselor's anxiety and his conflicted feelings be explored and that the dynamics in the client that deactivated him be tracked. The supervisor can help the counselor to regain his adequacy by helping him to search for the meaning of the impasse. Since an impasse in a counseling relationship is a consequence of a complex and subtle interaction between the counselor and his client, it follows that the process by which the supervisor enables the counselor to restore that relationship is an equally complex and highly idiosyncratic one.

We have often noted that clients with apparently similar dynamics can have varying effects on different counselors. Depending upon the client's conflicts and how they are expressed in the relationship, and depending upon the client's stimulus value for a counselor, different counselors may respond in varying ways to the client and develop quite different relationships. The supervisory process, then, can not be a process of generalizations alone. It must be a process that takes into account the reciprocal impact of a particular counselor and a particular client. In later chapters, we will exemplify the subtleties of differentiation that occur in supervision by demonstrating how individual counselors may respond differentially to clients and how the process of supervision may help each of them to be helpful in their relationship with these clients although counselors may bring different needs, strengths, and dynamics to bear on the cases and behave in multifarious ways with their clients.

COUNSELOR NEEDS
AND THE ENABLING PROCESS

Chapter 6

THE NEED TO UNDERSTAND CLIENTS:
GENUINE OR DEFENSIVE?

Counselors always have needs to understand themselves and their clients better. These needs to understand are often brought to the supervisory relationship. Initially, a supervisor often cannot differentiate what meanings the various counselor needs may have. However, as the relationship develops the supervisor may become increasingly aware that some counselor needs are genuine in the sense that the counselor incorporates supervisory help in a way which enables him to be increasingly effective with his clients.

At other times the supervisor may become aware that the counselor utilizes observations and suggestions in some way which is defensive for him and does not increase his effectiveness with clients. At such times a supervisor usually has a number of courses of action open to him. Which action or actions the supervisor follows are a function of his own personal feelings and perceptions and his own personal and professional life experience as well as

113

his present understanding of the counselor. A supervisor may react with anger, for instance, to discovering that a counselor is "copying" him or that the counselor is utilizing the supervisory relationship in some other way to defend himself inappropriately in his encounters with his clients.

We suggest that sometimes the supervisor's anger should be expressed. Such an honest expression may hurt, but it may also revitalize the supervisory relationship and even the counselor's relationships to his clients, since the expression is direct and will have an impact. It may even be discovered that the counselor has been angry with his own clients but has not known it. We are not advocating anger as a method of supervision; however, a supervisor does have feelings and he will find his feelings to be useful either through direct expression or through some dynamic understanding of their meaning.

Most often, we think, expression of feelings and a dynamic understanding by the supervisor of the nature of a given supervisory interaction combine to enable the counselor to be increasingly effective. We emphasize the probable importance of some direct expression of supervisor feelings because such expression makes the supervisor a human being who must be dealt with directly. Direct encountering with an appropriate affective base makes a relationship genuine and ultimately has the effect of reducing unrealistic or fantasied idealizing of the supervisor, thus reducing the utilization of imitative behaviors on the part of the counselor.

We believe, incidentally, that the manifestation of this behavior by a counselor reflects his own stage of psychological development. The need to emulate is real and perhaps must be understood and accepted for a time by a supervisor if it does in fact reflect an aspect of the counselor's development. The process of identification with significant figures should not, however, terminate with imitation; eventually it should lead on to internalization and incorporation of the supervisor as a significant person who is helpful and enabling but not restricting or binding. Finally, the counselor should be enabled to move on to independence and greater creativity; yet he should be ever mindful of his need for assistance when he encounters difficulties he cannot understand by himself.

Nurturance and Adequacy: complementary or antithetical?

Other counselor needs are experienced in relation to both clients and supervisors. The nurturant need to help others is, of course, generally an integral part of the personalities of counselors. The need is powerful and can and should be satisfied, in part, by relationships with clients who need nurturing. The power of the need and the nature of its probable development as a result of earlier interactions with significant persons, most often parents, can result in conflicted feelings and needs for supervisory help.

The very intensity of counseling relationships, the exacerbation of client symptoms, and questioning attacks by clients about the genuineness of the nurturant intent of a counselor can lead variously to counselors feeling angry, hurt, rejected, self-doubting, or challenged. At such times a counselor may deeply need his supervisor's help to understand better the sources and meaning of his needs to nurture. He may need, too, to understand more clearly why his client does not seem to be more receptive to his need to help.

A counselor, for instance, may become immobilized by self-doubt when his client questions the sincerity and genuineness of his motivation. This counselor may find in exploring his conflict with his supervisor that his client reminds him of a parent who demanded affection and was then scornful and rejecting when it was offered. Another counselor may feel angry, hurt, or rejected that his client does not seem to be accepting his eagerly offered help. This counselor may express at length that he has had much past success. His past success has perhaps been real but he may finally understand that his client is not so ready to accept and reward him as past significant others may have been.

A third counselor may be virtually paralyzed by his fears in his initial efforts at counseling. This person may speak of long and enduring needs to help others and also recount how very seldom he has been able to help. This counselor may finally be reminded of his mother who suffered greatly and that he could seldom, if ever, find ways to relate to her and help her to feel better. A male counselor may be disturbed by the client who, more or less subtly, suggests that counseling is more properly a feminine activity. Such a counselor may have reason to be disturbed since his father may have depreciated his efforts to be helpful as unmasculine.

Clients, then, can be threatening, even hostile, to the counselor's nurturant attitudes. When such threat occurs, it may be necessary for the counselor to explore and understand with his supervisor why he is threatened. The objective of the supervisor, however, is to free the counselor to be able to function effectively with his client rather than to resolve the counselor's conflicts. Continued recurring problems and conflicts with clients may, of course, powerfully suggest that a counselor may need more help than a supervisory relationship ordinarily provides.

Counselor conflicts about nurturance may be expressed in another way which may call for supervisory assistance. Frequently, a counselor's behavior in relationship to his clients may appear to be quite egocentric or even narcissistic. The counselor behavior in question will often be that of making rapid, perhaps insightful, and yet not very useful observations or interpretations to the client. In other words, the counselor's behavior is more ego-enhancing to himself than useful to his client. The counselor's conflict may surface in the supervisory relationship by continued seeking of approbation from the supervisor. Counselors legitimately need support and reward from supervisors, but repeated approval-seeking when coupled with egocentric behavior in relationship to clients suggests that the counselor's behavior should be explored and better understood. In fact, we suggest that the counselor's approval-seeking with the supervisor may well be the counselor's way of asking for help with his conflict.

When such conflicts are appropriately dealt with in supervision, we have noted that understanding the problem for the counselor often involves a realization that he experiences conflict between needs to nurture and needs to be adequate or potent. Put another way, the counselor may feel that if he is nurturant, he will lose his potency. On the other hand, he may also feel that if he is potent, he is not nurturant. Such a conflict may then result in a kind of counselor oscillation between nurturant efforts and misguided efforts to be potent. Freedom from the conflict may come fairly simply when the counselor is helped to realize the needs are not necessarily competing or conflicting and that neither his nurturant need nor his potency is seriously questioned by the supervisor. We have observed further that counselor behavior of the sort described is seldom truly narcissistic in the basic or primary sense. The behavior is usually rather far along the developmental ladder since much of the effort is to prove potency. The proof that the conflict is not a consequence of very early developmental problems comes when the counselor behavior fairly quickly modifies and changes when the problem is understood.

The Pain-Punishment Dimension

All counselor behaviors which utilize rapid, perhaps insightful, but not necessarily helpful interpretations of client feelings and attitudes, are not necessarily related to conflicts about nurturance and potency. Such behavior may also reflect counselor conflicts about a pain-punishment dimension in themselves and their clients. We believe that the experience of pain and hurt is a very frequent, perhaps necessary, concomitant of changing one's self. Counselors can become conflicted and confused, usually because of conflicts and dynamics of their own, when clients begin to experience or seem to be close to experiencing feelings of hurt and deprivation.

Clients, of course, are often quite sensitive to counselor conflicts and vulnerabilities about inflicting or causing pain in others. The counselor's conflicts may involve believing that the genuineness of his nurturant need is threatened by the client's experience of pain and hurt. The conflict may be exacerbated by the client's expressions which imply that his painful experience has been caused by the counselor who then may experience, in turn, anger, hurt, rejection, or even fears that the client is right.

The counselor's concerns may be further accentuated by his own introspections. The counselor's own increasing awareness of his own feelings and coincident increasing self-doubts may well include awareness that he has punishing feelings toward others. Further, he may even discover he has punishing feelings toward his client, and worse yet, that he may actually have been punishing to the client.

Such a state of affairs may cry out for supervisory assistance, but the counselor, because of the meanings he attaches to his own feelings and behavior, may need to conceal his conflict from his supervisor. Or, he may, because of other dynamic urges in himself along with his perceptions of the nature of the supervisory relationship, be led to confess copiously the nature of his error.

Neither counselor behavior is likely to be very helpful to either participant in the counseling relationship. The supervisor may however, still be of help. He cannot probably in the instance of the confessing, guilty counselor, absolve the counselor; but he can perhaps utilize the counselor's guilty feelings to arrive at better understanding of what has occurred in the counseling relationship. Although the counselor may believe that absolution by the supervisor may meet his need, we believe the supervisor may be of more help if he explores with the counselor what has happened between the counselor and client which has led to the guilt and conflict.

In the instance of the counselor who reacts to his increasing awareness of the painful experience of his client by concealing what is going on from his supervisor, the supervisor may discover the problem by another means. We add, parenthetically, that counselors who conceal a conflict or problem with a client usually must eventually seek help even though the need for help and the problem presented may both be distorted or disguised. The supervisor may note, when the counselor finally plays a tape recording of an interview with his troublesome client, that the counselor seems to be assisting the client in avoiding the necessary experience of pain or conflict by rapid, premature, although sometimes insightful responses to the client.

These responses may well seem to the supervisor to be intended to reduce or minimize feelings of anxiety, pain, or guilt rather than to expand them. The supervisor can, of course, react to his insight in various ways. He may react by being angry or punishing the supervisee, and this may be helpful although it may also serve the more doubtful objective of enabling counselor expiation rather than growth. He may pursue the counselor's need to conceal and this may also be helpful.

Ultimately, however, we believe that exploration into what has occurred in the counseling relationship antecedent to the present state of affairs is necessary. Counselors will perhaps be both relieved by the exploration and resistant to it, a response common to many people. However, as the supervisor's intent to help and facilitate continues to operate, the counselor's own need to understand will ordinarily be enlisted in the mutual search for the antecedent events.

As the antecedent events are clarified and understood, the counselor may even come to understand that his behavior has been punishing in a very different way than he has believed. He may find that his motivation to reduce pain and anxiety is ultimately more punishing than any punitive incident which has occurred. His anxiety-reducing behavior may actually prevent his client from experiencing his conflicts, expanding his feelings, and eventually finding better ways of feeling about himself and others.

IMPULSE CONTROL: WHOSE IMPULSES?

The expression and control of impulses in both client and counselor are often problems which call for supervisory assistance. Counselor behavior which is revealing of such a problem is often expressed in the interview by overt efforts to control the client's expressions and behaviors in content areas which may be meaningful to the client but are threatening to the counselor. Operationally, the counselor's behavior may again take the form of rapid, perhaps insightful comments about the client which may only serve to reduce the counselor's anxiety about his own impulses which the client's feelings and behavior have activated. The counselor's efforts to control may take the form of moralizing or judging. Such counselor behavior may at least, however, be direct in its expression and thus enable the client to defend himself in an equally direct fashion. The client may gain little help from such an interaction, but he is not likely to be hurt either.

We are somewhat more concerned about the counselor who has more clever ways of controlling impulsivity in himself and clients. This counselor, as we understand him, may control his own guilty feelings about his own impulses toward the client by subtly inducing guilt in his client. Cases involving attractive female clients and male counsélors perhaps best exemplify how inappropriate experiencing of guilt can occur. Female clients, of course, may develop sexual feelings toward their counselors. Such feelings may even be appropriate and necessary in order for the client to experience and to eventually resolve her conflicts. She will perhaps also necessarily experience guilt in regard to her sexual feelings.

Sometimes, however, the degree, duration, and the continuous alternation of sexual and guilty feelings may lead to supervisory puzzlement as to whose needs are being served. What may be finally discovered is that the counselor is being subtly seductive toward the client. His seductiveness stimulates the client's sexual feelings. Her experience of and expression of these feelings is, of course, satisfying in some way to the counselor since his own needs and conflicts have led him to be seductive in the first place. However, since the counselor has concern about and needs to control the direct expression of his own sexual feelings, he will have to act to control both his own feelings and his client's. The counselor's behavior and responses may then be directed toward the induction of guilt feelings in the client or the reinforcement and enhancing of guilt feelings already present.

Such counselor-client interactions can often be clarified and understood by tracking the sequence of responses in tape recordings of interviews. The client may first introduce sexuality by talking about her own feelings and conflicts in relationship to other men. The counselor will seem to respond with apparent appropriateness to the client's feelings although often he may seem subtly competitive or seductive. Gestures, voice tone, inflection, and choice of words may be utilized to further stimulate the client's feelings and perhaps to subtly direct the client's attentions toward the counselor.

So far, no error has necessarily been committed; and it may actually be that the relationship is developing as it must. However, as the relationship intensifies, both counselor and client may become conflicted about the present nature of their relationship and what eventual course the relationship must take. The client, for instance, may develop powerful guilt feelings about her past and present sexual feelings. She may also see and feel that the counselor is sexually available to her. Such feelings are also likely to provoke guilt in her.

The counselor, out of his confusion about his own feelings, may become quite conflicted as to how he should now express himself. In one way, the counselor may begin to assume inappropriate responsibility for the client's conflicts. He may even begin to think that he must and should be his client's sexual partner. Such a counselor conclusion, consciously or unconsciously experienced, necessarily grows out of the mixed motives with which he began the relationship or which have been activated by the flow of feelings and conflicts as the relationship has developed.

The counselor's conflict, then, grows out of his more or less conscious awareness that he wants both to help his client with her problems and to have sexual relations with her. The client may, of course, compound the problem by intensifying her own sexual feelings and may even make overt sexual demands; or she may withdraw or become increasingly guilty. Frequently, the client in her efforts both to work constructively on her problems and also to maintain the impasse in the relationship will go through an oscillating or cycling sequence of feelings—sexual, guilty, depressed, or whatever.

If the client continues her sexual intensification, her counselor, who has impulse problems, mixed motives, and a low level of awareness, will frequently desexualize the client by responding to and reinforcing the client's guilt. In so doing, the counselor may temporarily rid himself of his own guilt and conveniently now manage to see that the problem resides within the client. Yet the counselor's success in reducing the client's sexual appeal by inducing and reinforcing guilt, depression, and withdrawal may well activate the counselor's impulsive, seductive motive. He will then repeat with the client the cycle of seduction, intensification, guilt induction, and withdrawal.

We have often noted in our listening the dramatic switch in counselor response from sexuality to guilt. So also does the cycle of client feelings as described occur frequently. We wish also to emphasize, however, that counselor error does not in itself arise from the immediate consequences of impulsiveness and seductiveness. Such counselor motives and behavior may serve well to set a counseling relationship on an appropriate path. Seductiveness often cannot be behaviorally distinguished from warmth, interest, and a genuine motivation to help. It is only as the counselor experiences conflict about his motives that he may begin to confuse himself and his client. The guilt inducing behaviors and the consequent client cycling behaviors arise from continued counselor confusion and conflict. An impasse may be the ultimate result.

The supervisory process which facilitates counselor-client resolutions of conflicts resulting from problems in impulse expression is often complex. A number of supervisory courses of action are discernible and can be described. The supervisor, for instance, as a consequence of his own personal and professional experience as a counselor and supervisor may expect that most male counselors will have troubles with attractive female clients. Women counselors may have very similar problems with their male clients. Female counselors may often, appropriately enough it seems to us, feel more concerned about aggressive, hostile impulses in their male clients. Male counselors with male clients may well identify with and sympathize with their hostile, aggressive male clients rather than assisting these clients to experience, expand, and resolve their associated conflicts. Women counselors with women clients will, in the same way, often identify with their clients' impulses and their struggles to be women.

Even though a supervisor may be aware that the counselors he supervises will have problems with their own and their clients' impulses, his knowledge cannot ordinarily be immediately useful. He cannot, for instance, very well tell his male supervisee how to handle his relationships with women clients before the relationships have developed and are real. To attempt to teach in this didactic fashion may strip everyone—supervisor, counselor, and clients alike—of their adequacy to deal with problems as they arise. The very nature of human dynamics and conflicts dictates that they must be real and experienced before they can be understood and resolved.

So it is probable that the supervisor must hold the expression of his wisdom in abeyance until his supervisees actually begin to experience their inevitable conflicts and confusions. Along the way, however, the supervisor may note that his male supervisee comments often that his female client is unattractive. He may also observe to himself as he listens to the recording of an interview with his supervisee's client the counselor's behavior is warm and responsive—or is it seductive? He may also note that his supervisee has general concerns, moral or otherwise, with sexual expression—what does sex mean to him? Or the supervisor may note that the woman counselor he supervises seems preoccupied with male aggressiveness. Is aggressiveness sexual to her? Or is she herself aggressive? Perhaps she sees male aggressiveness in order to have a cover for her own seductiveness? Such supervisor wonderments may often be most tentatively held and go unexpressed for the time being. They may even be forgotten and recalled only when the supervisee begins to experience conflict, fright, or frustration and actively introduces his concerns into supervision. A counselor can often experience much support, help, and release from such a supervisor memory as they work together to understand the present dilemma.

In general, the supervisor functions in much the same manner with counselor-client impulse problems as he does in regard to other counselor and client concerns. The task is to assist the counselor to differentiate himself from his client by understanding himself, his client, and the nature of their interaction. A counselor may experience particular difficulty in differentiating himself from his client because the impulses and feelings experienced by both of them may be so powerful.

In our culture particularly, sexual and aggressive feelings often have special meanings which add to the potency of sexuality and aggression as sources of conflict. Thus such concerns are often overdetermined. Counselor and client may both be led to believe that the client's problem is sexual, aggressive, or both, with consequent exclusion of understanding, experiencing, and resolving other conflicts. Such an invariant view, despite the doubly determined power, may lead both counselor and client to feeling dissatisfied with their approach. Here the supervisor may assist the counselor to realize that the impulsive, attractive female client and the aggressive, hostile male client may both have associated problems about giving and getting affection from others.

These affectional feelings and conflicts are masked, in a sense, by the more clearly expressed sexual or aggressive problems. The counselor, with impulse concerns of his own, may well share with his client an underlying or associated conflict about the nature of affection and how one expresses or receives it. In fact, both counselor and client may be avoiding an affection or deprivation problem by concentrating on sexuality or aggression. Both perhaps may be acting impulsively in sexual or aggressive ways. Such impulsive "acting out" may thus rid the person of the threat of experiencing feelings of affectional deprivation or loss. The client's sexual and aggressive problems often diminish rapidly when the counselor, perhaps with supervisory assistance, is enabled to meet this client in a human encounter where both may know they have been and are deprived—yet they care about each other. Thus the counselor may come to know and understand that impulsive feelings in himself and his clients are not always as they may seem at first to be.

OMNIPOTENCE-IMPOTENCE: BIPOLAR?

All counselors want to feel adequate as human beings, as professional persons in a general sense, and, particularly, in relationship to their clients. Yet, often, the struggle to be adequate can so easily veer off into feeling omnipotent on some occasions or impotent at other times. Experienced counselors, as well as beginners and journeymen, can and do experience such disturbing feelings as a consequence of encounters with their clients.

Perhaps the search for adequacy can be characterized as an effort to stay on a highway which is bordered on one side by the beautiful and inviting "Omnipotence Mountains" and on the other side by terrifying "Impotence Cliff." Clients, of course, can and often do tempt counselors to climb to the mountain tops. Sometimes the counselor's own needs and dynamics can push him into mountain climbing. More often, the complex, subtle interaction of counselor and client dynamics together lead to counselor trips into the rarefied mountain air.

Yet the attainment of a mountain top may stir uneasy and

uncomfortable feelings. From a mountain top what direction is there to go except downward? The view to the bottom of the cliff below may be frightening and compelling. The trip down the mountain may well not stop at the highway. The momentum may carry our counselor on over the cliff where he will experience the crushing effects of inadequacy and immobilization. What is even worse is that there is no way back to the highway of adequacy.

Our topographic analogy suggests, then, that omnipotence may be a frequent and too often accepted temptation, while impotence lurks nearby as a more or less constant threat. The two states of feeling may appear to be, and perhaps are, the opposite poles of a semantic dimension. Psychologically speaking, we observe that the bipolarity may still exist. However, it also seems often that either feeling state carries the seeds of the other. Further, rapid oscillation between the two kinds of feeling can occur in such a short time span as a five minute segment of an interview. At other times, both feelings come very near to being experienced together. Thus, it happens that, while omnipotence and impotence may be semantic opposites, the experience of the feelings in counselors can rapidly fluctuate.

How can it be that counselors can seek, suffer from, and struggle with such feelings? The counselor's humanness, first of all, determines that he, as well as his client, is likely to be so affected at times. Each of us, in our own ways, is almost certain to have continuing needs and conflicts which will at critical times precipitate us into the glowing, expansive, yet uneasy feelings that are associated with omnipotence. While at other times, the same or other needs and conflicts will lead to the powerful feelings of inadequacy and terrible self-criticalness which are impotence.

Clients, too, often suffer from and struggle with the same problems and feelings. The interaction of client and counselor dynamics may lead to the experiencing of either or both states by both persons. Clients and counselors alike are sensitive to each other and either may utilize their sensitivity to promote or destroy feeling states in the other. For example, a client may quickly recognize that his counselor has powerful needs for his approbation. The client may well give his approval and the counselor may then enjoy consequent good feelings that he is very capable, perhaps even that he nears infallibility. The same client may then withdraw his approval or even become critical. The counselor may then feel angry, hurt, or impotent. He may even feel that he is at his client's mercy and that the client controls his feeling states—which may be very true in some ways. What the counselor does not have, of course, is a dynamic understanding of the nature of the interaction and that there is an understandable sequence of events which has led to such a state.

Another client may invite counselor efforts to help by passivity and apparent needfulness. Such client behavior and feelings should, perhaps, be responded to; and the client may respond positively to the counselor's efforts. The counselor's good feelings may grow and expand and he may believe, rightly in some ways, that he is being effective or even that he is ascending the mountain of perfection. Yet the same client, out of his own conflicts, fears, and angry feelings may become variously depressed, self-doubting, or critical of the counselor. Again, if the counselor has little understanding or awareness of his own and the client's needs, the meaning of the present interaction, and nature of the sequence of events in the relationship, he may well experience the terrifying fall into the angry, hurt, self-critical feelings which are inadequacy or impotence.

Inevitably, too, a client may come to realize that in some ways he controls his counselor's feelings of adequacy. Such awareness, at whatever level it occurs, may activate the client into uneasy omnipotent feelings also. The client may then, through his own internal workings or more likely through his continuing interaction with the counselor, find a way to return to his former passive, ineffective, impotent state. Thus, quite often counseling relationships can reflect the alternation of feelings of omnipotence, impotence, and sometimes even adequacy in both client and counselor. Such a curious, alternating set of feelings and interactions can be bewildering, frustrating, and inexplicable to both persons.

Oftentimes, such problems as we have just described cannot be avoided even though a supervisor has been constantly available and helpful. Further, we suggest that perhaps such problems must often occur in order for the client to experience himself and his conflicts genuinely. Also, in some ways, the counselor can only learn about himself, his clients, and the nature of the relationships he creates by behaving as his needs, dynamics, and conflicts dictate.

The supervisor may even find that his support, encouragement, and the behavioral freedom he may have facilitated in the coun selor have contributed to the impasse which the counselor eventually reports. Supervisors may feel and react in various ways to what has occurred. A supervisor who is concerned about his own adequacy may blame himself and even, psychologically if not actually, remove himself as an effective agent. Another supervisor with adequacy concerns may become hurt, angry, and punitive toward the counselor who has so badly used him. Neither of these supervisor reactions is likely to be helpful to anyone.

What the supervisor has lost sight of, or perhaps never really known, is that both supervisory and counseling relationships are genuine human encounters and that his adequacy, as with counselor and client, is earned over time and is not secured by apparent initial success. We believe that the wise, discerning, and differentiating supervisor will understand that he must be used in many ways by those he supervises. Also he needs to understand and believe that what is an impasse to client and counselor should not have the same meaning to him.

It is at the critical times when counselor and client may be harboring feelings of hopelessness about each other and their relationship that the supervisor may be most helpful. For one thing, the supervisor's attitude that matters are not hopeless provides an excellent beginning for resolving the impasse. But the supervisor needs to have more at his command than a belief or an attitude. He needs to have skills, knowledge, and understanding which can be communicated and utilized to help lift the counselor from his personal morass of despair and inadequacy.

How can this be done? What can the supervisor, in fact, concretely do which will enable his supervisees to deal more effectively with their feelings of omnipotence or inadequacy? We believe that in many ways each supervisor must find his own means for achieving this goal. But we also believe that there are some ways of proceeding which can be general guidelines to achieving adequacy as a supervisor.

First of all, the supervisor may need to examine his own relationship to his supervisee. He may well find attitudes and behaviors of his own which have contributed to the counselor's inadequacy. These behaviors, whatever they may be, should not, however, ordinarily be regarded as irrevocable supervisory errors any more than the counselor-client impasse would be regarded as irrevocable.

The supervisor should, we think, regard his behavior and its consequences as a valuable source of information which enables him to understand better himself, the counselor, their relationship, and the counselor-client relationship. The supervisor, too, can often begin to recall counselor behaviors and verbalizations which, while they may not have been explicable and usable at the time they were noted, can now be utilized. These recollections can facilitate supervisor-counselor exploration into the underlying nature of the counselor's own life with its conflicts, needs, and dynamics. This exploration necessarily continues to the point where the counselor's feelings of adequacy and his understanding of himself and his client are sufficient for him to return to the counseling relationship and act to revitalize it.

Eventually we believe that a supervisory relationship which has appropriately handled the problems of omnipotence, impotence, and adequacy as well as the other concerns which may have arisen, will enable the counselor to feel increasingly adequate. Further, we believe that ideally this relationship should become more equalitarian and consultative and less supervisory as counselor adequacy grows —the final objective being colleague status.

SUPERVISION
AND THE STUDY OF INTERACTIONS

Chapter 7

The process of supervision is based upon utilizing the resources of the counselor in order to enable him to activate or restore his relationships with his clients. The source of material for the supervisory sessions derives principally from the supervisee's encounters with his clients and secondarily from his supervisory relationship. The supervisory relationship itself is a human interaction process and as such the dynamics of the supervisee and supervisor are reciprocally affecting and changing each other.

The supervisor would be remiss if he did not make use of his understanding of the counselor's dynamics gleaned from his own contacts with him. And in this respect the supervisory relationship parallels the counseling relationship. The use, however, to which the supervisor puts this understanding and the extent to which he explores these dynamics with the counselor and thereby stimulates anxiety in the counselor is appropriate insofar as it has meaning to the counselor for his current behavior with his ongoing counseling cases.

Supervision necessitates the exploration of those counselor dynamics which have produced client change or those that have inhibited it. Impasses in a counselor's relationships often serve as a source of stressful material that the counselor brings to the supervisory relationship for assistance. At points of impasse, the counselor is often unable to reactivate a relationship because the impasse is itself a reflection of a critical encounter to which the counselor has responded inappropriately. The interaction of the dynamics of the counselor and his client that precipitated the impasse is generally subtle and complex and one that has existed for an extended period of time within the counseling relationship. As such, the counselor can get lost in the complexities of the relationship and may be unable to grasp the implications of the encounter.

Often a counselor will approach the supervisory relationship feeling inadequate, overwhelmed, confused, and possessing little insight into the meaning of the powerful feelings he is experiencing. The supervisor, in listening to the counselor describe the incidents that trouble him, in observing interviews, or through recorded materials can sometimes assist the counselor in recovering and restoring his adequacy with his client. The kinds of information that the supervisor may find useful and the ways in which he may employ it to achieve the goal of reactivating a relationship is the content of this chapter.

SUPERVISION AND THE RECIPROCAL IMPACT

In earlier chapters we have often said that similar client dynamics can elicit quite different responses in counselors. What the client attempts to elicit is a function of the stimulus value of this particular counselor on the client. What the client actually does elicit is contingent on the client's impact on the counselor. Hopefully, the counselor's responses are conditioned by the intention of helping the client to change. Therefore, we would expect that his responses would be anticipations of furthering the process of change. But the ideal is not always met; and counselors sometimes get so enmeshed in a relationship that change becomes remote, and the client's conflicts are reinforced.

The supervisor can help to unknot a relationship if he is a differentiating person who can respond to the client and counselor as two unique persons in conflict. By studying the interaction he may help the counselor to know more about what his dynamics are activating and how his client's behaviors are affecting him. Above all, the supervisor needs to believe that different counselors with varying strengths may each contribute something different to the resolution of clients' problems. What each of these different coun selors contributes to a client's ability to change is partly a result of the supervisor's being able to help each different person to differentiate himself from his clients.

The case of Miss Lorna helps us to examine the process of supervision and some of the dimensions of a supervisory relationship. Through this case we will demonstrate how several counselors who are dynamically very different people may actually encounter Miss Lorna and become incapacitated by her or mobilized to help her and the process by which a supervisor can assist counselors in differentiating themselves from a client.

The manifest content of Miss Lorna's conflicts reflected the subtly interwoven character of the underlying dynamics. It seemed apparent that Miss Lorna's developmental history must certainly reveal that she had learned early in life that her basic needs for affection could be satisfied only indirectly. The complicating layers of defenses that Miss Lorna had developed over time to disguise her basic needs from being recognized were most assuredly a measure of the threat that she experienced very early about expressing these needs openly. One may guess with some degree of accuracy that for her the threat of being abandoned must have been strong in order for her to construct the complicated and circuitous devices that she had developed in order to protect herself from having her wishes and feelings made known.

When Miss Lorna presented herself for counseling, it was equally clear that she had attempted to stamp out some of the potential danger to herself in her interpersonal relationships by being seductively demanding and yet hostile and threatening when anyone responded to the demands by being either sexual or nurturant toward her. Apparently, when others were responsive toward her, their behavior was reminiscent of earlier promises of help which she had responded to only to encounter punishment. Nurturant behavior of others toward her seemed to carry the threat that she might be stimulated to reach out and be hurt again; so her response to a nurturant approach to her was usually to draw back and defend by hostile counterattack. Her initial presentation then was one of attempting to be wily with the counselor and yet to be explosive and bitter if he moved toward her.

Different counselors may respond to Miss Lorna in very diverse ways. One counselor may respond to the challenge of working with her. His response may really be a mixture of a wish to be nurturant and helpful mixed with curiosity about the delicate intertwined nature of Miss Lorna's conflicts and what the process of helping her to change would be like—a curiosity that is at once touched with the challenge of the scientist to understand human behavior better and the hope of the humanist to uncover and revitalize her humanity.

Other counselors may respond to Miss Lorna by being threatened by her. A counselor's response to her may be dynamically determined by his own feelings and conflicts regarding the layers of defenses that Miss Lorna has constructed to protect herself. The counselor may respond to one of her defensive layers as though this were all of Miss Lorna and the defense may be so emotionally charged for him that he is overwhelmed. For example, he may respond to the threat of attack by a female, and this threat may have to do with his own conflicts about angry women. Another counselor may be threatened by Miss Lorna for a different reason. His response to her may have been governed by countering Miss Lorna's seductiveness with seductive feelings of his own. His own anxiety may have been stimulated because his seductive feelings toward the client were met by hostility, and his own fantasies about her may make him feel guilty and immobilize him from working with her. On the other hand, the client's hostility may further challenge the counselor to activate the relationship as a form of sexual encounter.

Another counselor may respond to the double message that Miss Lorna is communicating. Although Miss Lorna may actually have learned the double message for one reason, her counselor may be responding to it in accordance with his own dynamics. The counselor may have in his own past history been bound up by a significant female who invited his affection and then punished him for it. Still another counselor may feel threatened by Miss Lorna because he experiences her basic hollowness and the depth of her deprivation more intensely as a result of his own deprivation. His is a sympathetic communication; he identifies with the client because he feels deprived.

SENSITIVITY AND SUPERVISION: DIFFERENTIATION REVISITED

In the case just cited, each of the counselors who approached Miss Lorna did so by responding to something about her that they experienced in their relationship with her. We can probably safely assume that all of the counselors were stimulated by cues that Miss Lorna emitted and that they were not solely responding to their internal stimulations. In a sense, then, all of the counselors were sensitive. Yet, in some cases, the counselor's sensitivity would not be helpful in developing a good counseling relationship. Undifferentiated sensitivity, then, as a relationship concept would not seem to be a useful one in evaluating the potential strength of a counselor. The task of the supervisor should be to help to differentiate the counselor's sensitivity in relation to its effectiveness in furthering the relationship. Otherwise, sensitivity, like adequacy, can be a double-edged sword.

Sensitivity has a number of dimensions to it, and the supervisor can help the counselor to differentiate his sensitivity by understanding the dynamic meaning of it. Sensitivity can consist of the counselor's responding to minutia in the client as though these minor components of the client's conflicts were the client. Such counselor behavior can only be confusing to the client since he must continually feel that the counselor is not reaching him; yet since the counselor does periodically brush the periphery of his conflicts, he must feel some promise of eventual help. We have observed that counseling relationships in which the counselor is hypersensitive to details which have only the remotest connection to the major conflict often are of little help in changing the client. The counselor who, defensively it seems to us, fixates on detail generally labors the specifics of the content while the major affective struggle is bypassed.

A counselor's sensitivity may also be reactive in a negative sense. Here again the counselor's response may be accurate but not helpful. In this case, the counselor's own conflicts and sensitivity activate his anxiety and incapacitate him. When the counselor's sensitivity is reactive, it generally means that his own internal stimulation is so strong that the counselor misreads the client's dynamics because something about the client triggers his anxiety and overwhelms him. Reactivity can be a useful counselor characteristic, however, if the counselor can be helped to understand his reactions and then to translate his reactions into better understanding of his client and the nature of their interaction.

One of the hypothetical counselors who responded to Miss Lorna was so intensely stimulated by the client's hostility because of his own feelings about angry women that he was unable to respond to her further in a therapeutic way. Miss Lorna was angry; so in that respect the counselor was sensitive. But the counselor's sensitivity was incapacitating to him because it was associatively close to his own conflicts and he was flooded by his own internal stimulation. In effect, the counselor projected his own conflict onto Miss Lorna and anticipated responses from her that derived from his own fears.

Sensitivity in both of these last instances reflects a similar consequence. The counselor is perceptive to something that emanates from the client, but he is unable to convert his experience into a productive relationship. In the first case the counselor tuned in on such a microscopic wave length that the majority of what he picked up had little meaning for the client. In the second case the counselor was accurate but his vision was tunneled by his own conflicts, and whatever he sensed was interpreted from a highly personal framework.

How helpful the supervisor can be with these counselors depends on a number of things. One of these counselors may be experiencing anxiety which is largely situational. The counselor may experience some threat of being evaluated. The supervisory-learning situation may be the source of a part of the counselor's anxiety and may contribute to his hypersensitive feelings. This counselor may be someone who has had relatively little experience in the process of counseling or of being supervised. We would guess that, in this case, after the counselor has gathered strength from successfully working with some clients, he may eventually be more productive.

Whether the counselor whose sensitivity activates his own conflicts can be a good counselor depends in part upon whether he can tolerate his anxiety in the relationship and bring it to the supervisory relationship without having needed to reduce the anxiety at the expense of the client. In other words, the fact that the counselor's anxiety stirs up his own feelings may not critically differentiate the good from the poor counselor so much as whether the counselor can "sit on" his anxiety long enough to examine its meaning. If the counselor can sustain himself in the relationship and stave off his need to reduce his anxiety immediately through rapid interpretations or insightful statements or some such device which wards off the affective struggle with the client, then the supervisor may be able to help him to differentiate, control, and utilize the sensitivity that activated the anxiety.

A counselor's anxiety at times arises from the counselor's fears that the client and he have the same problem. The counselor's fears that the client's problems are his own problems is often a fallacious conclusion drawn from the rather shaky premise that the problems are the same because both the client and he have some common overlays to their problems. The client may utilize ways of coping with others that are similar to the counselor's and the counselor may assume that the coping behavior has the same dynamic meaning for them both. Or, the circumstances surrounding the client's developmental history may be similar to the counselor's own history, and the counselor may inappropriately conclude that both he and the client have interpreted their experiences similarly. The supervisory process may consist of helping the counselor to differentiate the premises from the conclusions.

Supervision and Restoration: tracking the critical events

One of our hypothetical counselors responded to Miss Lorna's seductiveness and hostility in another way. He felt guilty for being seductive himself and was immobilized. When this counselor enters a supervisory relationship he may only know that he feels uneasy with the client. The supervisor may choose any one of a number of courses in order to reestablish the counseling relationship. It may be necessary for the supervisor to help the counselor to regain his adequacy by helping him to track the sequence of events in the relationship that immobilized him. Sometimes when a counselor approaches his supervisor for help in restoring a relationship, the supervisory task may consist of looking at the counselor's and client's most recent behavior as a mirror of what the relationship is like and what needs to be done to revitalize it. It may be enough that the two of them examine a "snapshot," a recent critical incident which precipitated the impasse, but more intense and extensive explorations of the nature and meaning of the impasse may be needed. The counselor and supervisor may actually need to track an entire sequence of events because the impasse may reflect the end point of the client's reenactment of an entire phase of his developmental crisis.

The question of how intensive and extensive an exploration of the counseling relationship the counselor needs, can use, and will use is partly a function of what the supervisory relationship is like. If the supervisee experiences threat of punishment in the exploration of events which disabled him, he is unlikely to regain his adequacy. The most that the counselor may gain from such supervision when he is feeling guilty about his counseling relationship is some feelings of expiation for his counseling behavior.

The supervisor, in punishing the counselor for his counterseductiveness with Miss Lorna, relieves the counselor's guilt without using the guilt to explore the dynamics which activated it. The consequences of such expiation without insight are that the impulse is not brought under control. Without much doubt, the impulse will seek expression at the next opportunity. The supervisor's punishment then does no more than reinstate the counselor in the relationship so that he can recreate the same insatiable cycle by sexualizing the relationship again, leading to further guilt and need for expiation. Unfortunately, Miss Lorna will have learned little from the relationship that is unique, and she will have reconfirmed old omnipotent feelings about the power of her sexuality.

Provided, however, that the supervisor does not use the relationship to punish the counselor for his counseling behavior and that he communicates some support in the counselor's search for the dynamics that immobilized him, the relationship may be reactivated. The process by which the supervisor tracks the dynamics which deactivated the counselor is challenging and emotionally taxing to both participants. The essential objective in the search is to help the counselor spell out the dynamics on both sides of the picture. Whether the counselor can do so depends, as we have said, to a large extent on the supervisor's feelings about him. If the supervisor attitudinally and behaviorally supports the counselor in his quest and communicates some hope to the counselor that he will be able to disengage himself from what has been disabling him with his client, then the counselor will take the risk of exploring the meaning of the impasse. Perhaps we can demonstrate some of the subtle differences in supervisory attitudes which may make the difference in whether the counselor is reactivated by referring again to the case of Miss Lorna.

One of our counselors was threatened by Miss Lorna because he experienced a "push-pull" in his relationship with her. From the counselor's point of view, he felt an attraction for the client, but when he responded by approaching her, Miss Lorna lashed out at him. When this counselor entered supervision, he had little knowledge of what threatened him about Miss Lorna. He reported that his feelings seemed to be bound up somehow. In his relationship with her, the counselor said that he oscillated between wanting to help the client and "freezing" at critical moments. He indicated further that his own wish to help was almost simultaneously countered by feeling that he would be overpowered by the client. Over time, the counselor reported that his concern had mounted and both he and the client had been considering terminating the relationship.

These feelings in the counselor had become critical since he felt that his own angry feelings about the client's behavior with him were stirred up enough so that he did not see how he could be effective. The long standing and recurring disabling events in the relationship, his feelings that the task was impossible, and the way in which he and the client seemed to be continually binding each other are all supervisory cues which support the supervisor's intuition that in the relationship the client is experiencing and acting out with the counselor the generic conflict.

The supervisor is now confronted with several alternatives. He can blame the counselor for fulminating the client's conflicts and suggest to the counselor that he has committed a number of therapeutic errors. Such supervisory behavior would most certainly increase the counselor's anxiety. The counselor would experience the supervisor's punishment and would probably return to the relationship with renewed anger that was aggravated by his being "reprimanded" by the supervisor. If we assume that the counselor's initial anger toward the client was displaced from earlier relationships, his additional feelings of frustration from his supervisory relationship will act as a bellows on that anger and the client will inevitably be doubly punished for experiencing her conflicts.

We might assume quite accurately that the supervisor's behavior with this counselor derives in part at least from his own anxiety that a counseling relationship over which he has supervisory responsibility has gone awry. In the same way that we feel that good and poor counselors can be differentiated—not by their anxiety but by what they do with that anxiety—so we would feel that the supervisor may need to "sit on" his anxiety and consider the mental health of his supervisee rather than his own adequacy.

What the supervisor probably needs to remember is that the very purpose of a therapeutic relationship is to permit and facilitate the client's experiencing of his conflicts. Only by experiencing conflicted feelings that have been hidden away and by reawakening the affect that has been compressed can the client hope to change. The critical dimension here is that the experience of the conflicted feelings must occur under different learning conditions than the earlier experiences in which the client learned the inappropriate behaviors. We would propose, therefore, that therapeutic error does not reside in the fact that the counselor has fallen into the trap of behaving like the earlier significant persons that were causative agents of the conflict; rather the therapeutic error resides in confirming—that is reinforcing—the conflicts within the counseling relationship.

It is essential that the supervisor be able to distinguish between the fact that this counselor in his relationship with the client triggered the conflict by his behavior but is not the causative agent of the generic conflict. If the supervisor takes the position with the counselor that this triggering process and activation of the conflictual experience is a necessary antecedent to resolving the conflict, then the supervisor may free the counselor to study the dynamics in both the client and counselor that have activated the conflicts in the relationship.

It has been our observation that when the supervisor punishes the counselor for triggering conflicts and not understanding what has been activated, a therapeutic error will occur in that the counselor is then often unable to regain the adequacy necessary to correct the client's emotional experience; and the relationship terminates with both participants feeling badly. We feel in many cases that it has been the supervisory attitude rather than the counselor's error that has prevented recovery and contributed to the counselor's failure.

The supervisor has several sources of information which can be useful to him in understanding what has occurred in his supervisee's relationships. From the report of the counselor of his discomfort with the client, from the counselor's description of the client's dynamics, and from the counselor's own behavior in the supervisory relationship, the supervisor can begin to track the meaning of the impasse. By incorporating the counselor's feelings about the case into the information gleaned from the recorded interviews, the supervisor and counselor can probably reconstruct some of the critical incidents in the client's development which have contributed to and determined her interaction with the counselor.

Miss Lorna's development reflected the fact that in her early contacts with significant persons she had been offered affection and then punished for it. The counselor and supervisor could relate this inconsistent behavior to her interactions with her father. The father was apparently drawn toward the client with a genuine wish to nurture her, but when he did approach her, the father would sexualize the relationship. Although other explanations may be equally applicable, we may assume that the father was frightened by his own feelings because he would then withdraw from the relationship and act in cold, distant, and punishing ways toward the child. In seeking her father's affection and in experiencing his sexual demands that were packaged with having her own affectional needs met, Miss Lorna herself may have begun to experience the relationship as a sexual one. After all, the lesson she had learned from her father was that his basic need was a sexual one and that unless she fed these needs her own needs for affection and security would go unmet. In experiencing the relationship as a sexual one, Miss Lorna may have complemented her father's seductiveness with sexual fantasies of her own toward the father; so that his punishment may have been experienced by her as something she deserved.

The promise of being nurtured by a male then would carry with it the threat that the relationship would be sexualized. In fact, it would be felt as an essential adjunct to affection and perhaps even the sole avenue to getting affection. But such sexualization would consequently terminate in punishment. The supervisor can probably infer quite accurately that the counselor's nurturance toward Miss Lorna is interwoven with seduction and that the client is countering with seduction of her own. These conditions are also partly responsible for triggering the client's and counselor's frustration, anger, and threats of terminating the relationship.

The fact that the counselor may play into the client's conflicts is revealing of his own dynamics and conflicts. Passages of recorded material may be sufficiently anxiety-provoking to the counselor to confirm the supervisor's feelings that the counselor has not differentiated his need to help the client from his wish to be seductive. In addition, the case may also reflect something of the counselor's own problems which led to his feelings of being bound by the client. In his relationship with the counselor, the supervisor may need to help the counselor to know something of his seductive feelings toward the client. Secondly, the supervisor and counselor may need to explore the counselor's overreactivity to a female who promises receptivity but then threatens aggression.

Here again the supervisor's attitude toward the counselor can be a punishing one. The supervisor can teach the counselor that his seductive feelings toward the client are bad and that his feeling "bound" by the client is a sign of weakness in working with female clients. Our view would be that the supervisor can work with the counselor to explore enough of himself and what these dynamics mean to him to permit him to "unbind" himself with the client. It may be that in their exploration of the case, the counselor may gain some emotional insight into his own reasons for behaving like the client's father. The counselor's own attraction and fears may be reminiscent of his experiences with significant females in his own past where he may have been drawn to them and then punished.

Our feelings about supervision as an enabling process suggest to us that exploration of the counselor's dynamics which inhibit his counseling relationships is inevitable. We feel that such exploration will occur when the supervisor's attitudes as reflected in his behavior are that he wishes to help the counselor to restore his relationships. How extensively the counselor explores his own dynamics with the supervisor is governed by their purpose in working together, and that purpose as we have repeatedly said is to facilitate the supervisee's ongoing counseling relationships.

IDENTIFYING AND FACILITATING APPROPRIATE TERMINATIONS

Counseling relationships terminate in many different ways. Much research effort has been devoted to determining or differentiating the success or failure of counseling efforts. In many ways these research findings have been equivocal insofar as defining clearly when a counseling relationship has been a success or a failure. Certainly there are many problems in defining the criteria which are a clear indication that clients have changed in a way which is desirable.

We suggest, as others have before us, that the problems are indeed complex and that disagreement about outcome criteria may well continue. It is even probable that what is success in terms of one way of theorizing or viewing counseling process and outcome may well be failure when viewed from another vantage point. We suggest, too, that what may be failure to one counselor may be success to another. As we have suggested many times throughout this book, clients with apparently similar dynamics and conflicts are often quite different from each other. For these apparently similar and yet ultimately different persons, we have indicated that the process of counseling should follow and develop the idiosyncratic ways in which each person has lived his own life, developed his own conflicts, and become himself whatever that self may be.

In our view, then, the problem of determining counseling success hinges significantly on at least two ways of viewing human beings. In one way each of us, more or less in common with at least some of our professional colleagues, formulates a norm for desirable human behavior which may run as a common motivating thread through all or most of our counseling relationships. Thus, each of us, may wish to help our clients to learn that we all are human beings who share likenesses or similarities with each other. Such feelings of sharing with and being like other human beings are, we think, essential to being human. Few people relish the sense of abandonment or isolation which a lack of sharing of common human experience may entail. Promotion and development of feelings of being like, sharing with, and giving and getting interactive rewards from other human beings is a legitimate counseling objective.

Yet most of us, counselors and clients alike, may recoil with some shock or even fright when we note that being like other human beings may smack of conformity. At such a point, each of us in our own ways, may begin a more or less frenzied search for the way or ways in which each of us is unique and like no other human being. Often we observe that the search for either human likeness or uniqueness may be frantic, rebellious, or even outright injurious to one's self and others. Adolescence and early adulthood may often epitomize the sometimes desperate efforts to be commonly human on the one hand and uniquely human on the other. Further, these needs are often felt to be antithetical and contradictory. But we would suggest that these human needs are not necessarily contradictory and that both kinds of goals are appropriate for counselors to effect. In fact, we would suggest that one way in which a counseling effort is successful is the degree to which the client can experience both his uniqueness and his commonness and further, that each way of feeling is an acceptable, valued part of himself.

If our way of viewing human beings has truth, then the problem of measuring human attributes at all is complex and must involve both these aspects of humanness. So, too, must assessment and evaluation of counseling processes and outcomes take account of these two aspects of human nature, as well as other views of the qualities of humans. Our research, then, into the mysteries of counseling may necessarily yield different results from study to study. So too do our measuring instruments differ and correlate positively in one situation and negatively in another. Perhaps the degree to which studies or measuring instruments agree reflects the amount of common humanness each may have studied or measured. On the other hand, disagreements between researches or instruments may only reflect the human uniqueness being studied or measured.

If our way of viewing human beings has meaning, then counseling processes, outcomes, and terminations should reflect these dual aspects. We believe that our descriptions and explications of counseling and supervisory processes have reflected our concern with both commonness and uniqueness. At some points, appropriately we hope, we have emphasized one aspect rather than the other. We have spoken more of uniqueness than commonness yet we affirm our belief in the importance of both.

How, then, do counseling relationships terminate? How do the dual aspects of human nature express themselves at termination? Neither aspect may express itself particularly or clearly. Sometimes one or the other aspect predominates. In the instances of nonexpression of either aspect we suspect that the counseling relationship may not be very successful. Terminations which involve broken appointments or failure to return for leavetaking or mutual agreement to terminate often suggest to us that the experience has been a failure for client, counselor, or both.

It is worth noting that beginners at counseling more often have terminations which may involve the client's failing to return to terminate. Why should this be? Lack of skill is, of course, often the reason. Yet we suspect that another even more dynamic reason may be often involved. Inexperienced counselors, the more experienced on occasion also, usually experience high levels of anxiety about themselves as persons, their skills as counselors, and high concern about forming relationships. In fact, the beginning counselor or the counselor with strong feelings of inadequacy may well seem to be concerned only with whether his clients will return to see him.

In other words, the counselor's concern is not with change and development, but with getting the client to like and approve of him. In fact, success for many beginners is often measured by the fact that a client or clients keep returning. When the counselor's motivation is as described, perhaps the client may see his only alternative as breaking appointments or failing to return. It is as though the client must express his uniqueness by breaking off the relationship without thanks or mutual agreement.

The most appropriate termination, as we view it, is one where there is mutual agreement that the counseling relationship has served its function. At such a time the affective storms have subsided and client and counselor feelings about each other have been relatively stable for a period of time. The client usually reports, often with wonderment, that he is different and that people are responding differently to him. The client frequently says that he feels change will continue or that problems may still arise but that he believes in his ability to deal with both the present and future.

Concomitantly with the development of such client feelings comes the first tentative expression of wishes to be independent of the counselor. These wishes may often be balanced by wishes to "keep the door open" and wishes for assurance that return for further help is acceptable to the counselor if the client should have the need. It is most often at these points, where the client begins to express his tentative need to separate or feels that he can deal with his problems, that the counselor may need supervisory guidance.

At termination time, the counselor may not recognize the meaning of his client's behavior. Perhaps counselor nonrecognition of the possible meaning of such client feelings and behavior relates most often to the fact that the relationship has had and still has deep meaning and satisfaction for him. The counselor may actually be reluctant to recognize the client's feelings since to do so means that he will lose closeness and contact with someone who is meaningful and rewarding to him. Yet termination must come and the supervisor may help with the recognition but not with the actual termination. Termination of a meaningful relationship must be accomplished by the participants themselves. Finally, client and counselor will come to a full recognition, separately in many ways perhaps, that they have meant and will continue to have importance to each other. Then they can agree to separate with awareness in each person that they are commonly human. Yet each of them is unique since genuine sharing has led to autonomy.